1123 HARD TO BELIEVE FACTS

by

Nayden Kostov

1123 HARD TO BELIEVE FACTS

by

Nayden Kostov

Luxemburg
2016

1123 HARD TO BELIEVE FACTS
first edition

Author: Nayden Kostov
Editor: Jonathon Tabet
Design: Yuliya Krumova
Format: 5,25 x 8

ISBN-13: 978-9995998011
ISBN-10: 9995998017

Contents

PROLOGUE

Following the success of my website www.RaiseYourBrain.com and numerous inquiries from readers, I decided to collect the best gems of breath-taking trivia and to present you a great compilation of facts, suitable for a vast and diverse audience. This is a result of years of sifting through history and references books on a myriad of subjects as well as searching the Internet and paying attention to the news.

Apparently, this book can be fun for high-school students too– even the most 'spicy' entries, neatly separated in the chapter 'Facts about human and animal sexuality', remain factual and abstain from profanity. To my greatest delight, an avid reader of my site explained that she was preparing daily fact sheets for her son's lunch box. She prints out three facts every day to create some lunch-time fun for her child and thus entice him into further reading and to provoke his intellectual curiosity. Honestly, I wish my parents had done the same for me when I was a child!

I confess that most trivia books are insufferably boring. This inspired me to write a book which is different, packed with interesting, educational, and fun ingredients; it seeks to entertain as well as to challenge. It will provide you with never-ending intellectual ammunition for a lifetime of dinner parties. You will amaze your friends and family by recounting to them that the greatest Chinese pirate of all times was a woman, or that herrings use flatulence to communicate!

The book will be your strongest ally in combatting social awkwardness and will arm you with plenty of icebreaking pieces of trivia, suitable for any occasion.

CHAPTER 1

Unbelievable facts about virtually everything

1.

In many Israeli schools, algebra is taught without the use of the symbol '+', as it looks like a Christian cross. They use an inverted 'T' instead (see below).

2.

Mercury is the planet closest to the sun and yet is not the hottest one in our solar system. Venus, the second closest planet, is in fact far warmer.

3.

Chewing gum, yoga and poorly-made dental fillings make you flatulent.

4.

The words 'gym' and 'gymnastics' both derive from the Greek word for 'naked'.

5.

'Karaoke' means 'empty orchestra' in Japanese.

6.

In a classic deck of cards, the king of hearts is the only one without a moustache.

7.

What we refer today as Arabic numerals actually originated in India. In Arabic, they are known as 'Indian numbers'.

8.

Sudan has far more pyramids than Egypt.

9.

In the black and white TV era, female anchors used green or black lipstick.

10.

One of the most frequent regrets of those on their deathbed is: 'I wish I hadn't worked so hard'.

11.

Pope Francis was a bouncer in his youth.

12.

Fucking is an Austrian village (see below) where the beer 'Fucking Hell' is produced ('hell' means 'clear' or 'light' in German).

13.

There are about 50 million kangaroos in Australia, more than two for every Australian.

14.

The moon and the sun appear to be the same size due to the coincidence that the moon is 400 times smaller and 400 times closer than the sun.

15.

The first product to have a bar code was Wrigley's chewing gum.

16.

'Goodbye' originates from 'God bye', which came from 'God be with you'.

17.

McDonald's began as a hot dog stand.

18.

The first official match of the NBA (the men's professional basketball league in North America) was not played in the USA. It took place in Toronto, Canada, on 1 November 1946, with the Huskies hosting the New York Knickerbockers.

19.

Today, there are more Uber cars in New York City, USA, than there are yellow cabs.

20.

The 17th Prime Minister of Australia, Harold Edward Holt, disappeared on 17 December 1967 and was never seen again.

21.

Solariums are outlawed in Australia and Brazil.

22.

Mr. Smith-Cumming was the first director of the British Intelligence service, MI6. Ironically, he introduced a method of using semen as invisible ink.

23.

Ketchup originates from China.

24.

Bicycle was invented after the steam-powered locomotive.

25.

If the speed of evolution of Intel microprocessors (since 1971) had been applied to cars, in early 2016 one car would have cost five cents and would have travelled faster than light.

26.

In 2002, the US Congress acknowledged that an Italian immigrant, Antonio Meucci, was, in fact, the real inventor of the telephone, some 20 years ahead of Alexander Graham Bell.

27.

In the 1990s, Super Mario was better known to US children than Mickey Mouse.

28.

Victoria's Secret catalogues were initially sent to men only.

29.

When flying from Tokyo, Japan, to Hawaii, USA, you can arrive the day before you departed.

30.

The sound of a whip crack is actually the sound of the whip's tip breaking the sound barrier.

31.

Gerald Ford served as US president and vice president without being elected to either post.

32.

Whittier is a town in the state of Alaska, USA. The vast majority of its population lives in one single building.

33.

France is the country with the most time zones in the world. However, Russia has the largest number of contiguous time zones.

34.

There is liquid water on Mars.

35.

In the 1970s, the three best-known western names in China were: Jesus Christ, Elvis Presley and Richard Nixon.

36.

At one time, the Soviet Union was spending over 40% of its GDP on arms.

37.

Humans suffer from cancer much more often than whales and sharks do.

38.

Helicopters are the safest means of air transportation.

39.

Amongst the 10 busiest container ports worldwide, six are located in China.

40.

Cuttlefish ink was used in early photography.

41.

Electronic payments are leading to a cashless society. An unexpected benefit is that bank robberies in the USA have fallen by 40% in the course of the last 10 years.

42.

There are more lakes in Canada than in the rest of the world combined.

43.

Frank Oz is the voice behind both Yoda and Miss Piggy.

44.

It's possible to travel by boat from Pakistan to Russia if you sail in a completely straight line.

45.

On average, astronauts are 5 cm (2 inches) taller in space.

46.

Christianity, Islam, Hinduism, Buddhism and Judaism all started in Asia.

47.

Isaac Newton died a virgin.

48.

Long ago, the phrase 'mad as a hatter' was used literally. Hatters used mercury in their work, which made them go insane.

49.

Due to the Earth's rotation, an object will go slightly further if thrown towards the west.

50.

The Icelandic government developed a smartphone app to curb involuntary inbreeding. With a population of just 332 000 people, the chances of meeting a cousin at the bar are quite high.

51.

Ernest Rutherford used to say that 'All science is either physics or stamp collecting'. Ironically, he was honoured with a Nobel Prize in chemistry.

52.

Sometimes Pluto comes closer to Earth than Neptune.

53.

In Yellowstone Park, USA, there are many more hot springs and geysers than in the rest of the world.

54.

There are almost 800 million $2 bills in circulation worldwide – they are anything but rare!

55.

Arsenalna station in Kiev, Ukraine, is the deepest metro station in the world – almost 106 m (346 feet) below street level.

56.

In 2015, an abandoned airport in Spain was sold for €10 000 ($11 000). It cost €1 billion to build and was operational only for a single day.

57.

The US stock market always dips around the date of a sun eclipse.

58.

Musical notes got their names from the first syllables of each verse of the religious hymn 'Ut Queant Laxis' (see below).

Ut Queant Laxis (Hymn to St. John the Baptist)

Guido of Arezzo
(circa 991-1033)

Translation:

So that your servants may, with loosened voices, resound the wonders of your deeds, clean the guilt from our stained lips, O Saint John.

59.

'For sale: Baby shoes, never worn' is considered to be the shortest novel ever written.

60.

Tommy Atkins serves as a generic name for a British soldier; in the US Marine Corps, it's Lance Corporal Schmuckatelli.

61.

Torpedoes were named after a fish species.

62.

The superstition 'three on a match' or 'unlucky third light' dates from the Boer War, when sharpshooters often killed the third enemy soldier lighting a cigarette from the same match at night.

63.

The surface of the moon covers roughly the same area as Asia.

64.

Most restaurant menus have at least 100 times more bacteria on them than the toilet lids in the same restaurant.

65.

In the years 1600 and 2000, there was a 29 February; in 1700, 1800 and 1900, there was not, nor will there be in 2100.

66.

Since 1945, all British battle tanks have possessed tea-making equipment.

67.

Nazi Germany introduced the torch relay, which transports the flame from Greece to the respective site of the Olympic Games.

68.

Licking 10 postage stamps burns 1 calorie. You will not lose weight however because the adhesive contains starch.

69.

In China and Japan, some women wear special hairy stockings to deter rapists.

70.

In ancient times, salaries were paid in salt (hence, the origin of the word).

71.

All the gold in the world, extracted since the dawn of humanity, would fit into a cube with sides of just 20 m (65 feet).

72.

Airbags inflate in just 30 milliseconds.

73.

There are more than 300 million ping-pong amateur players in China.

74.

The first commercial flight of a jumbo jet was made in 1970.

75.

Buildings in China and Hong Kong rarely have floors containing the digit '4', as it sounds like the word 'death' in Chinese. Naturally, nobody wants to live there.

76.

Alexander Pushkin, the 'Russian Shakespeare', was the grandchild of an Ethiopian slave.

77.

In some cases, male urine can turn a pregnancy test positive. In fact, it may be an indication of testicular cancer.

78.

Both marine vessels and aircraft have green lamps on the right side and red ones on the left.

79.

The safest seats in an airplane are at the back, aisle not window, and closest to emergency exits.

80.

Bluetooth was named after the Danish king, Harald 'Bluetooth' Gormsson, who lived in the 10th century.

81.

George W. Bush was, in fact, a male cheerleader in college.

82.

'Yo Mama is so...' jokes started among African Americans before their emancipation from slavery. 'Mama' was used as a code word for 'Master'.

83.

Tracy, Hilary and Shirley used to be boys' names.

84.

On 3 September 1939, France declared war on Germany, and the French troops were the first to cross the border.

85.

The Hundred Year War actually lasted 116 years.

86.

Most 'paper' banknotes are made of cotton.

87.

The owner of the Segway Company died riding a Segway.

88.

Platinum was only discovered in 1735. Until then, it was thought to be 'fake' silver.

89.

In 1960, the strongest earthquake on record occurred in Chile. It had a magnitude of 9.5 (out of 10) on the Richter scale.

90.

The letter 'J' is not used in the periodic table of elements.

91.

In some US states, women and black people had the right to vote as early as the 1790s.

92.

90% of the volume of fresh snow is air.

93.

In 2012, Costa Rica outlawed hunting.

94.

In 1943, the entire crew of the destroyer USS W.D. Porter was put under arrest. Why, you might wonder? It almost sunk President F.D. Roosevelt's ship. Twice.

95.

Actually, Christopher Columbus never set foot on mainland North America.

96.

The brands Puma and Adidas were founded by two brothers.

97.

In the USA, deserters from the Vietnam War are still being tracked down and arrested.

98.

Google Street View blurs the face of Colonel Sanders in each KFC logo because 'he was a real person'.

99.

There is no hospital in Vatican City.

100.

St. Patrick was, in fact, not from Ireland.

101.

Pluto was discovered, declared a planet and then had its title rescinded before even making it half way around the sun.

102.

Nepal is the only country to have a non-rectangular flag (see below).

103.

The state of Alaska is 425 times larger than the state of Rhode Island, USA.

104.

According to the 1872 Licensing Act, it is illegal to ride a horse while drunk in Great Britain.

105.

Selling and using chewing gum in Singapore can result in fines and jail time.

106.

The highest mountain in our solar system is on Mars.

107.

Ebola survivors should use condoms for the rest of their lives as the virus is found in semen months after recovery.

108.

I bet you did not know that Winnie the Pooh was named after the bear 'Winnie' and the swan 'Pooh'.

109.

In most families, there are fewer photos of the second child than of the first one.

110.

Never heard of Xiaomi? It is the third largest mobile phone producer in the world.

111.

During World War II, US soldiers and German Wehrmacht soldiers once fought together against SS troops.

112.

Buzz Aldrin was the first man to urinate on the moon.

113.

Taphophobia is the fear of being buried alive.

114.

Bubble wrap was initially supposed to be marketed as wallpaper.

115.

'Senator' means 'old man' in Latin.

116.

Less than 10% of all inmates in US state and federal prisons are women.

117.

According to the US Bureau of Justice Statistics, in 2014, Oklahoma had more than a 10 times higher female incarceration rate than Rhode Island.

118.

The 'Playboy' magazine was initially meant to be called 'Stag Party'.

119.

The countries Lesotho, Vatican City and San Marino are enclaved states. This means that they are completely surrounded by the territory of another, larger state.

120.

In some parts of Switzerland, flushing the toilet after 10 pm is against the law.

121.

The Nazis abandoned the Gothic script in 1941 as it was too hard to read for the majority of German citizens.

122.

In 1941, Hitler prohibited smoking in most public areas.

123.

The Republic of Nauru has no capital city.

124.

‘Samsung’ means ‘three stars’.

125.

All Middle Eastern countries except Lebanon have a desert.

126.

Water is densest at 4ºC (39.2ºF).

127.

There are military airplanes equipped with 105 mm howitzers.

128.

The company Asus was named after Pegasus.

129.

Nintendo started business in the 19th century, initially selling playing cards.

130.

In each of his movies, Tom Cruise has a scene where his hair is wet.

131.

18 countries, the largest being Saudi Arabia, don't have a single river.

132.

The word designating 'butterfly' is unique in the majority of languages.

133.

The words 'bet', 'drug' and 'puke' were all introduced into the English language by Shakespeare.

134.

Self-guided 'smart' bullets already exist.

135.

The brand name JEEP evolved from the army abbreviation for 'General Purpose' vehicle – G.P.

136.

In the Westminster Parliament, UK, the Speaker of the House cannot speak (express an opinion).

137.

There are flying skateboards. In 2015, the company HENDO created a working prototype, just like the one from the movie 'Back to the Future'.

138.

The most faked artist in the world is Salvador Dali.

139.

White and yellow cars are less likely to be passively involved in a car accident.

140.

Lucky Strike cigarettes refer to the gold rush in which everybody dreamt of striking gold.

141.

In the solar system, Venus is the only planet to turn clockwise.

142.

Zebras in warmer climates have more stripes.

143.

The greatest Chinese pirate of all times was a woman named Ching Shih (1785-1844).

144.

Other than its derivatives, 'dreamt' is the only word ending in 'mt'.

145.

Edible packaging for foods has already been developed.

146.

The inventor of the electric chair was a dentist by profession.

147.

A roulette wheel in Rio All Suite Hotel and Casino in Las Vegas, USA, once stopped seven times in a row on the number '19'.

148.

The F-104 fighter jet (photo below) was nick-named 'Aluminium Death Tube' and 'Widowmaker' for a reason. The German Air Force lost 269 aircraft (roughly 30% of its entire F-104 fleet) and 116 pilots died, all in peacetime.

149.

A Listerine mouthwash advertisement coined the phrase 'always a bridesmaid, never a bride'. The message was that if you have bad breath, nobody would marry you.

150.

The entrance door at 10 Downing Street (the residence of the UK Prime Minister) can only be opened from the inside.

151.

Several countries used to have nuclear cannons and howitzers.

152.

The guillotine was named after a French doctor. His descendants changed their family name out of shame.

153.

In 2004, the former Soviet republic of Georgia spent three months without traffic police.

154.

The first living creatures to fly in space and come back alive were fruit flies. They were sent up in a modified trophy Nazi V2 rocket in 1947.

155.

The front edge of some military jets' wings is as thin as a knife (less than 0.5 mm or 0.02 in.)

156.

Over 27 000 North Koreans have defected to South Korea since the 1950s.
Only several dozen South Korean citizens fled to North Korea during the same period.

157.

Japanese Sokushinbutsu sect members mummify themselves while still alive. The practice is banned in Japan.

158.

The producer of mummy brown pigment stopped production in the 1930s when he ran out of raw materials, i.e. Egyptian human and animal mummies.

159.

During the War of 1812, soldiers misinterpreted the 'U.S.' abbreviation on their 'U.S. Beef' rations, thus coining the phrase 'Uncle Sam'.

160.

Nodding your head expresses 'yes' in the vast majority of cultures. Be careful though – it means 'no' in Bulgaria.

161.

The NATO member Iceland has no army.

162.

San Marino and Sweden were foes during the Thirty Year War (1618-1648). They signed a formal peace treaty officially ending the conflict in 2004.

163.

One of the language choices when using ATMs in Vatican City is Latin.

164.

DNA analyses support the theory that more than 2000 years ago one legion of the Roman Army lost a series of battles and its descendants ended up settling in China.

165.

Mickey Mouse's white gloves were initially meant to make his hands visible in early black and white movies.

166.

Listerine mouthwash was initially sold as a floor-cleaning substance.

167.

Serbia, Macedonia and San Marino are all landlocked countries but participate in the Mediterranean Games. Israel does not.

168.

Historically, in many North American cities, 1 May used to be ‘moving day’ and the only possible date on which one could change dwelling.

169.

As of mid-2016, the Phantom of the Opera is the longest running Broadway show, with almost 12 000 performances.

170.

In 2013, a single tuna fish was sold in Japan for $1.76 million.

171.

A widely used green wall paint, containing arsenic, was to blame for the poisoning of thousands of people in the 18th and 19th centuries, including, allegedly, Napoleon Bonaparte.

172.

In a single battle in modern day Germany (Battle of the Teutoburg Forest), the Roman Empire lost three legions (around 20% of its total manpower).

173.

The US company OPENBIOME is willing to pay $13 000 (over €10 000) a year for your faeces. It uses them for faecal transplants.

174.

Robes became the standard outfit for English judges around 1350, during the reign of Edward III.

175.

Brussels became the ‘capital’ of Europe because Belgium, in alphabetical order, was the first country on the list. At the time, it was thought to be a temporary solution.

176.

In 1987, seven million US children disappeared overnight. How? The Internal Revenue Service stopped the widespread fraudulent practice of listing phantom children for tax exemptions.

177.

The carrousel was initially used by the French military for basic cavalry training.

178.

The Mars rover, Curiosity, was equipped with the strongest parachute ever built by mankind. It worked perfectly and ensured a soft landing on the Red Planet.

179.

Initially, tuna was advertised as ‘chicken of the sea’. Its taste was unknown to the general public. The marketing ploy, which implied similarity to something familiar, worked just fine.

180.

In 1897, Amos Dolbear formulated a relationship between the rate of cricket chirps and temperature.

181.

A triangle can have 3 right angles if drawn on a sphere.

182.

According to Cunningham’s law, the best way to get

the right answer on the Internet is not to ask a question but to post a wrong answer.

183.

In antiquity, a Greek city would demolish part of its fortress walls after one of its citizens had won the Olympic Games. Its rulers believed that 'with such citizens we have no need for walls to feel protected'.

184.

Doing your favourite activity temporarily boosts your IQ.

185.

A €3 coin is in circulation in Slovenia (see below).

186.

Blue street lights in Tokyo, Japan, and Glasgow, UK, successfully led to a drop in crime and suicides.

187.

There is an escape tunnel leading from the Pope's inner chamber to a place beyond Vatican's borders.

188.

Picasso is the artist with the most stolen works. As of mid-2016, over 1000 of his paintings are missing.

189.

In 1952, Einstein declined an offer to become the President of Israel.

190.

Iceland does not have a single McDonald's restaurant. It does not have a Starbucks café either.

191.

Al Capone's tailor made the clothing for Robert de Niro in the movie 'The Untouchables'.

192.

In Dubai, United Arab Emirates, it is possible to withdraw gold from a special ATM.

193.

In ancient Rome, Julius Caesar's contemporaries celebrated Lupercalia, a festival that is thought to be the forerunner of our modern Valentine's Day.

194.

H.L. Hunley was a submarine of the Confederate States of America and the first combat submarine in the world to sink a warship.

195.

A malignant melanoma was discovered in Bob Marley's toe and doctors suggested an amputation. He refused for religious reasons and died of cancer.

196.

Birthday paradox: in a group of only 23 people, there is a 50% chance that two of them share a birthday.

197.

In 1712, there was a 30 February in Sweden.

198.

One in six residents of Singapore is a millionaire in US dollars.

199.

The most destructive earthquake ever occurred in 1755. It completely destroyed Lisbon, the capital of Portugal.

200.

On 23 January 1556, the deadliest earthquake in history killed about 830 000 people in Shensi, China.

201.

When clearing the 9/11 debris, workers discovered a renaissance merchant ship.

202.

Edwin Booth, a brother of Lincoln's assassin, saved the life of the President's son in a train accident.

203.

In public toilets, the urinal closest to the door is always the cleanest one.

204.

The invention of the salt dispenser was inspired by the way poppies eject their seeds.

205.

The sun is considered red in Japan.

206.

Forget what you read in books – the moon has no dark side.

207.

People who are incredibly beautiful get, on average, fewer dates because they are perceived as too hard to approach.

208.

In 1967, Sweden changed from driving on the left side (UK style) to driving on the right side (continental style). The very first day, as was to be expected, the traffic was totally disrupted (see below).

209.

'Tokyo' literally means 'eastern capital'.

210.

Buildings, streets and pavements in central Chicago, USA, were physically raised with hydraulic jacks in the mid-19th century.

211.

In 1967, the Republic of Benin proclaimed independence. It only lasted a few hours.

212.

Brennender Berg (Burning Mountain) is a deserted coal mine in Germany that caught fire in 1688. It is still burning.

213.

Graham Island (close to Sicily, Italy) was once mistaken for a submarine and was attacked with depth charges by US fighter jets.

214.

The strong chemical smell from a swimming pool actually indicates that there is not enough chlorine in the water.

215.

The introduction of boxing gloves actually increased the number of fatal incidents.

216.

Visitors to Antarctica usually remove their appendix in advance of their trip as there are few doctors on the continent able to carry out the procedure in the event of appendicitis. Bonus fact: In 1961, a Soviet doctor successfully removed his own appendix at Novolazarevskaya station, Antarctica.

217.

There are silent discotheques, where visitors use wireless headphones.

218.

Dark green is the best colour for blocking UV rays.

219.

The idea of a space elevator was conceived in 1895.

220.

At the end of winter in Luxembourg, they burn an enormous wooden cross in a tradition called Buergbrennen.

221.

In the USA, as of early 2016, the state of Alabama has the highest percentage of believers, New Hampshire - the lowest.

222.

Fictitious telephone numbers with the prefix 555 are widely used in movies. However, some real 555 numbers do exist.

223.

The Cox–Zucker machine is, in fact, an algorithm created by David Cox and Steven Zucker.

224.

The continent, America, was named after Amerigo Vespucci, who actually visited it after Columbus. Columbus, in turn, was predated by the Norse Vikings, who visited Newfoundland centuries before.

225.

Viral videos do, in fact, spread following the same pattern as infectious diseases.

226.

There are confirmed cases of people who ate poppy

seeds and then had false positive results for opium on drug tests.

227.

Muphry's law states that: 'If you write anything criticising editing or proofreading, there will be a fault of some kind in what you have written'.

228.

In most amnesia cases, recent memories are always the most affected.

229.

Kotooshu, one of the most successful Sumo wrestlers of all time, was born in Bulgaria (see below).

230.

Jack Daniel's last words were: 'One last drink, please!'

231.

After months of research, scientists in Yokohama, Japan, came up with the conclusion that 'people who think they have foot odour do, and those who don't, don't'.

232.

Homer did not use the word 'blue' in 'The Odyssey'. There was no proper word for blue in ancient Greek.

233.

20% of the world's construction cranes are in Dubai, United Arab Emirates.

234.

Since 1989, it has been illegal to buy laboratory glassware in the state of Texas, USA, without a permit.

235.

The tyres of heavy mining vehicles are often filled with sand.

236.

A study has revealed that, statistically, rich people position their toilet paper with the free end up. According to the same study, poor people do the opposite.

237.

While in Sweden, most American and British tourists are tempted to photograph 'Slutstation' public transport signs.
Actually, in Swedish, it simply means 'end station'.

238.

Every year, Curiosity (the robotic rover on Mars) plays itself the song 'Happy Birthday'.

239.

In ancient literature, honey was described as being green.

240.

In 1993, the state of Michigan, USA, legalised watching television while driving, provided that a special image projection device is used.

241.

The euro is also a legal tender in some parts of North America. It can be used in the French departments Guadeloupe, Martinique, Saint Barthélemy, the Collectivity of Saint Martin, Clipperton, and Saint Pierre and Miquelon.

242.

Recently, a diamond the size of the moon was found in space. It was called 'Lucy', a tribute to Beatles' song 'Lucy in the Sky with Diamonds'.

243.

Beer bubbles comprise mostly nitrogen and carbon dioxide.

244.

Up to 10% of narco-dollars, kept in secret warehouses, end up damaged by rats.

245.

The construction of the International Space Station has so far cost almost $160 billion, making it the most expensive single man-made object.

246.

The four rings on the Audi car logo represent the four founding companies.

247.

'Inemuri' is the Japanese equivalent of siesta. It is quite acceptable in the working place.

248.

The thick atmosphere and low gravity on Titan, one of Saturn's moons, make it theoretically possible for people to fly by flapping small wings attached to their arms.

249.

From space, the sun appears white.

250.

Ferdinand Porsche, the founder of the Porsche car company, did not receive a university education.

251.

Samsung is also a car manufacturer.

252.

The Austrian Zwentendorf nuclear power plant cost €1 billion to build but did not run even for a single day, due to the outcome of a referendum.

253.

According to eyewitness accounts, Escobar's drug cartel used to spend $1000 a week on rubber bands to wrap up all the cash.

254.

Every time a military jet lands on the wrong aircraft carrier, it is a tradition to cover it with graffiti before sending it on its way.

255.

San Marino, founded in 301, is the oldest constitutional republic. Its borders have not changed for the last 8 centuries.

256.

France, Israel, Spain, and Italy have passed laws prohibiting fashion models from looking anorexic.

257.

There is a Kremlin (meaning fortress) in many Russian cities, not just in Moscow. Novgorod, Tula, Kazan and Smolensk, for example, all have their own one.

258.

Since 1933, the winners of the Indianapolis 500 automobile race receive a bottle of milk of their choice.

259.

The largest building by volume is the Boeing factory in Seattle, USA.

260.

In Munich, Germany, you can purchase a classy 30-minute stress-relief session for €139 ($150). You are given a baseball bat to destroy a fully equipped sham office.

261.

The AK-47 was based on the StG 44, a German SS assault rifle from 1944.

262.

The world's most polluted city in 2014 and 2015 was Delhi, India.

263.

By 2017, Norway will stop broadcasting analogue FM radio stations and will only use digital radio.

264.

The designer of Volkswagen Golf, one of the most successful passenger cars of all times, first offered the prototype to FIAT, which turned it down for being 'too ugly' (see below).

265.

In 1970, Keith Emerson recorded the first lead synthesizer solo.

266.

If Buckingham Palace were ever put on the market it would be the most expensive residential property worldwide.

267.

Wind generators with horizontal turbines are more efficient than those with vertical ones.

268.

Since 1958, half a billion hula hoops have been sold worldwide.

269.

For a couple of decades in the 19th century, ice was the second biggest US export, after cotton.

270.

The domain 'symbolics.com' is thought to be the first .com ever; it was registered on 15 March 1985.

271.

In 1975, Gary Dahl sold over 1.5 million 'Pet Rocks' and became a millionaire. A Pet Rock was, in fact, just a smooth stone in a cardboard box.

272.

Shanghai Tower is China's tallest building at 632 m (2073 feet).

273.

In early 2015, Apple was twice the size of the second biggest S&P 500 company. The last time that the largest company was twice as large as the second one occurred in the 1980s.

274.

In Las Vegas, USA, baccarat earns more money than blackjack, poker and craps combined.

275.

On several occasions, bitcoin experienced over 1000% volatility.

276.

The 'Super Mario Bros.' series holds a Guinness record for being the 'most successful gaming franchise of all times'.

277.

There is frozen water on Mercury.

278.

The Hague, The Netherlands, and Luxembourg City, Luxembourg, have exactly the same statue of King William II in their city centres.

279.

Annually, up to 11 000 Europeans die prematurely due to noise pollution.

280.

According to a ruling of the General Court of the European Union from 2015, Skype's name is too similar to that of the broadcaster, Sky, and the public is likely to be confused. This effectively blocks the registration of Skype's logo and trademark in the EU.

281.

Jupiter is heavier than all other planets of our solar system combined.

282.

There are many manganese nodules measuring 20 cm (8 inches) in diameter in the Atlantic Ocean. The reason for their existence remains unexplained.

283.

A magazine once deliberately used ink mixed with HIV-infected blood in an attempt to challenge the AIDS stigma.

284.

You need a Chinese driver's licence to drive in mainland China.

285.

The plant *Pandanus candelabrum* grows in diamond-rich soil only.

286.

In 2000, the Millennium Bridge in London, UK, stayed open for only three days before a complete overhaul was needed as it swayed heavily in the wind.

287.

80% of the active substances in US pharmaceutical drugs are manufactured abroad.

288.

Vancouver, Canada, used to have a floating McDonald's restaurant.

289.

The kite experiment was a scientific experiment proposed by Benjamin Franklin. The experiment itself was first performed in France.

290.

Until recently, 98% of DNA was thought to be ‘junk’ DNA as it does not contain genes.

291.

Drought led to the demise of Mayan civilisation. Ironically, evidence for that was found 120 m (400 feet) underwater.

292.

A forest in Germany has the shape of the swastika when seen from the air (see below).

293.

The legal driving age in El Salvador is 15.

294.

At any point in the lower 48 states in the USA, there is a McDonald's restaurant less than 200 km (110 miles) away.

295.

FIFA has more member states than the United Nations.

296.

There are wind turbines without blades which have been proven to be more efficient than those with.

297.

The sun is responsible for the water cycle on Earth, which makes hydroelectric power indirectly linked to solar radiation.

298.

The airplane Convair B-36 was unique in many aspects: combining a record number of 10 propeller and jet engines, it had the longest wingspan and was the largest piston engine aircraft ever built (see picture).

299.
In 2013, a car was melted by sunrays reflected from a London skyscraper. After the accident, the building was called 'the Walkie Scorchie'.

300.
Vakkaru Island in the Maldives is almost entirely made up of fish faeces.

301.
The ancient Spartans used a cyphering tool called 'Scytale'.

302.

When a lightning strikes nearby, the electrostatic potential between a cow's legs causes a shock that often kills them.

303.

Most modern CPR dummies have the face of an unidentified girl who drowned in the Seine River, Paris, France, at the end of the 19th century.

304.

Riding a bicycle with a helmet makes car drivers subconsciously drive closer to you.

305.

Forest fires can travel at speeds of up to 22 km/h (14 mph).

306.

Romania has the biggest salt mine in Europe.

307.

Centralia, Pennsylvania (USA), has been burning for the last 54 years. A coal mine underneath the town caught fire in 1962 and shows no sign of abating.

308.

Interstate 180 in Wyoming, USA, is only 1.75 km (1 mile) long.

309.

On most maps from the 16th and 17th centuries, California is wrongly depicted as an island.

310.

Historians never used the concept of year 0 (zero). Contrary to common logic, year 1 BC was followed by 1 AD.

311.

Being afraid of the number '13' is called 'triskaidekaphobia'.

312.

In 1963, a modified F-104 fighter jet reached an altitude of 36 km (119 000 feet).

313.

Peanut butter is effective for cleaning chewing gum that is stuck to your hair.

314.

In 1958, the greatest tsunami ever recorded happened in the state of Alaska, USA. It was 524 m (1720 feet) tall.

315.

The Pauli effect describes the unexplained and repetitive failure of technical devices occurring in the presence of the Austrian physicist Wolfgang Pauli.

316.

Atacama Desert, Chile, is one of the driest places on Earth.
In October 2015, however, it was literally flooded after it received rainfall of 25 mm (1 inch) in a single day.

317.

In 1939, the Black Friday Bushfire in Australia annihilated a territory about the size of Israel.

318.

Labour costs in Denmark are 10 times higher than those in Bulgaria. Both countries are part of the European Union.

319.

The last minute of 30 June 2015 had an extra second.

320.

US student loan debt has surpassed $1 trillion. That exceeds all credit card balances due in the country combined.

321.

There is no vegetation in the so-called Fairy Circles of Namibia and nobody knows why (photo below).

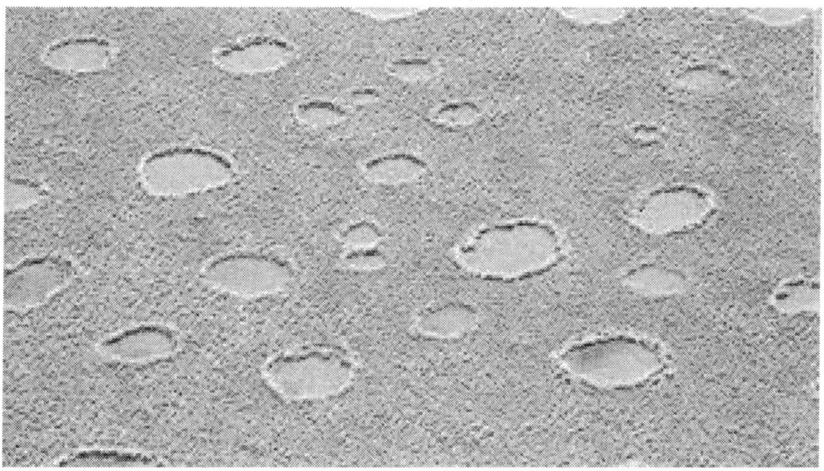

322.

Relatively late in life, the actor Jack Nicholson found out that his elder sister was, in fact, his mother.

323.

In the US presidential elections, it is estimated that the winning candidate could cut his campaign budget in half and lose only 1% of the vote.

324.

Nördlingen is a German town that is located inside a crater formed by the impact of a meteorite.

325.

Americans spend $2 billion every year on chewing gum.

326.

Snail massage of the face is very popular in Thailand and South Korea.

327.

Belgium issued a commemorative 2.5 euro coin to mark the anniversary of the Battle of Waterloo. The irregular denomination prevented France from legally blocking it (both countries are in the Eurozone).

328.

At the Battle of Waterloo, only 33% of Wellington's troops were British.

329.

Dimpled golf balls fly twice as far as non-dimpled ones.

330.

Since 2011, Hungary has been destroying GMO crops located within its territory.

331.

In 2015, a primary school in the UK banned handstands and cartwheels for safety reasons.

332.

Sunset on Mars appears blue.

333.

Belgium once could not form a government for almost two years.

334.

There are artists who use their own blood for painting.

335.

Constructed 80 years ago, the concrete in the middle of Hoover Dam (USA) is still hardening.

336.

Levi Strauss never wore a pair of his own brand jeans.

337.

The Magellanic Clouds are, in fact, two irregular dwarf galaxies, visible from the southern hemisphere. At the time, Magellan kept wondering why those clouds did not move.

338.

The beer 'Corona' is marketed in Spain as 'Coronita' because the Spanish royal family are the trademark owners of 'corona' (Spanish for 'crown').

339.

90% of people think that when they use humour in emails, the recipient will understand. According to studies, only 56% of recipients actually get the joke.

340.

Three out of every 10 foreign tourists visiting the USA choose New York City as their destination.

341.

In the 1950s, the FBI investigated Albert Einstein for espionage.

342.

Germany will convert more than 60 obsolete military bases into wildlife reserves.

343.

There are three vehicles abandoned on the moon. They cost over €30 million.

344.

In 1996, the Venice opera burnt down because the firemen had no water!

345.

Porcelain was invented in China over two millennia ago. Europeans learned how to produce it in large quantities only in 1710.

346.

The Internet evolved from a secret military project called ARPANET.

347.

Employees in administration spend 52 minutes a day, on average, dealing with emails.

348.

For over 200 years, Ceres, with its diameter of 950 km (590 miles), was the largest known asteroid (see below). In 2006, it was reclassified as a dwarf planet alongside Pluto.

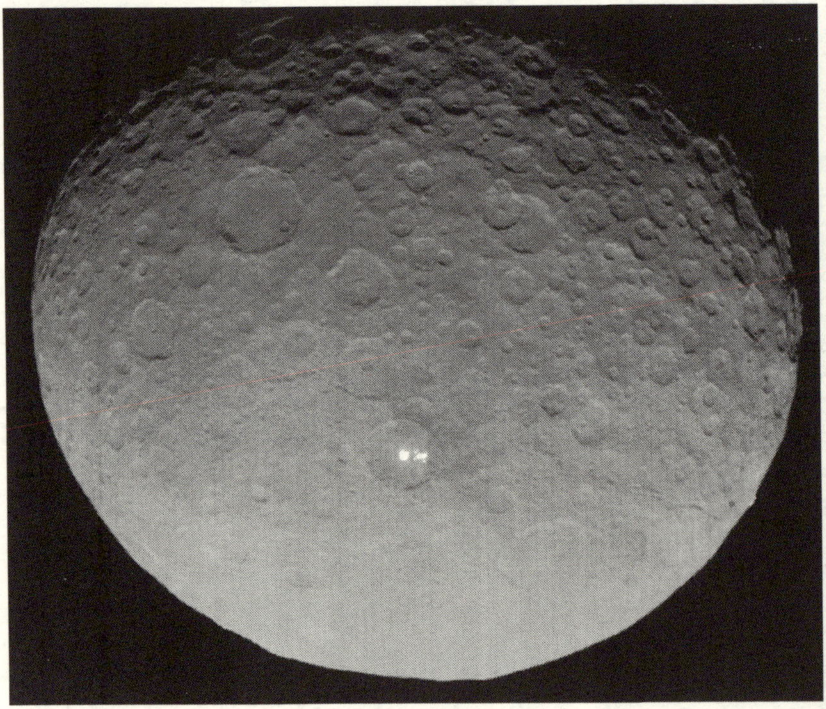

349.

Should we colonise Mars, at certain moments, communications would be tricky. At the maximum distance from Earth, radio waves would need 23 minutes to travel in one direction.

350.

The best telescope on Earth can detect candlelight on the moon.

351.

It is impossible to belch in zero gravity.

352.

In 1984, Michael Jordan was the third pick in the NBA draft.

353.

The smog in Beijing, China, is often visible from space.

354.

Owing to quite strange circumstances, the US soldier, Joseph Beyrle, served a couple of months in the Russian Red Army during World War II.

355.

The word ‘hooligan’ only appeared 130 years ago.

356.

The Cambrian period was named after the Latin name for Wales.

357.

The first astronauts were supposed to escape from the rocket with a zip line should something go wrong during the launch.

358.

So far, the only US president to have visited a federal prison is Barack Obama.

359.

Diving suits were initially designed for firefighters.

360.

Naval artillery takes into account the rotation of Earth.

361.

Charles Darwin and Abraham Lincoln were born on the same day.

362.

Aluminium used to be considered more precious than silver.

363.

Selling alcohol at sports events has actually been proven to decrease the number of alcohol-motivated misdemeanours.

364.

Taxonomy deals with the classification of species into categories. For decades, there was not a single taxonomist in Africa.

365.

If a single cell reproduces itself, and each new cell in turn reproduces itself 50 times, the final number of cells will equal that of the cells in your body.

366.

Venezuela claims two thirds of the territory of neighbouring Guyana.

367.

In 1816, there was no summer. A massive volcanic eruption from the previous year ejected so much dust into the atmosphere that it cooled down the entire planet.

368.

Despite being an island, Australia imports seafood as most of its adjacent waters are very poor fishing grounds.

369.

The chances in golf of scoring a hole in one (an ace) are estimated to be 1:12 000.

370.

India bans any movie showing a person smoking.

371.

In Japanese, 'karate' means 'empty hand'.

372.

Every year, the moon moves about 4 cm (1.5 inches) further away from Earth.

373.

North Korea banned the movie '2012' because they had their own prophecy for that year. Both prophecies were wrong.

374.

Dmitri Mendeleev was inspired to create the periodic table of elements by a game of Solitaire.

375.

Charles Darwin did not use the word 'evolution' in the first five editions of the 'Origin of Species'.

376.

A major airline seat manufacturer has patented rows of seats which alternately face towards the front and back of the plane.

377.

If Earth had no liquid iron core and hence no magnetic field, it would be subjected to deadly space rays and life would be impossible.

378.

Mars's liquid core cooled down and almost entirely solidified. This resulted in the disappearance of its magnetic field.

379.

There are only three dozen atoms of francium on Earth.

380.

Any spaceship that were to penetrate our atmosphere at an angle greater than 5.8 degrees would, most probably, burn up on entry.

381.

Worldwide, less than 50 people are actively looking for asteroids.

382.

Shortly after publishing his Theory of Relativity, Albert Einstein was turned down for the post of a high school teacher.

383.

In Greek, 'asteroid' oddly means 'similar to a star'.

384.

A nuclear bomb unleashes only 1% of all the potential energy locked in the uranium.

385.

Professional astronomers often measure distances with the unit 'parsec' (approximately 3.26 light-years).

386.

At any given moment, there are around 100 lightning strikes occurring simultaneously around the world.

387.

All the clouds combined contain less than 0.01% of all the potable water on Earth.

388.

The eastern coast of the Pacific Ocean is 45 cm (1.5 feet) lower than the western one due to the rotation of Earth.

389.

We have more detailed maps of the moon and Mars than of the bottom of the oceans.

390.

Coral reefs host 25% of all fish species.

391.

Carl Wilhelm Scheele discovered eight chemical elements but received virtually no recognition.

392.

The astronomer, William Henry Pickering (1858-1938), thought that the black spots on the moon were migrating insects.

393.

After withdrawal of lead-containing fuel from the market, the lead in our blood dropped by 80%.

394.

Each time you start a fluorescent lamp, you split the atom.

395.

The Soviet Union drilled a hole 12 262 m (over 40 000 feet) deep and called it ‘the well to hell’.

396.

The Great Hadron Collider has magnets that weigh more than the Eiffel Tower.

397.

An asteroid nearly missed Earth in 1993. It passed only 120 000 km (75 000 miles) away.

398.

'Mastodon' means 'nipple tooth' in ancient Greek.

399.

At the edge of our solar system, the sun is not the brightest star.

400.

If all the clouds rained down at once, it would only raise the level of the oceans by 2.5 cm (1 inch).

401.

The state of Florida and the southern part of the state of Texas are the safest places in the USA concerning earthquakes.

402.

The inventor of the electron microscope received a Nobel Prize 54 years after his invention.

403.

Engineers in the oil business knew decades before geologists that continents move sideways.

404.

Iceland is situated on both the European and American tectonic plates.

405.

In the 1970s, small plutonium cells were used in implanted heart pacemakers.

406.

Jimmy Carter was the first US president to be born in hospital.

407.

'Molecule' roughly means 'extremely minute particle'.

408.

The first webcam was utilised to observe a coffee box.

409.

You cannot touch anything – the electrons in your hand and those in the object will maintain a tiny distance between themselves.

410.

In 1808, Humphry Davy discovered an element and called it aluminium. Four years later, he renamed it to aluminum, hence, the two forms of the word.

411.

According to NASA, 98% of matter was created within the first three minutes after the Big Bang.

412.

Real estate ads containing '!' should be avoided. Experts confirm that the presence of an exclamation mark is usually linked to concealed information or a distorted description.

413.

On 15 January 1919, a great part of Boston, USA, was covered with molasses in what is known as the Great Molasses Flood. 21 people died and 150 were injured (see picture).

414.

Unlike in the USA, conservative parties worldwide typically use the colour blue.

415.

There are no skyscrapers in central Paris, France,

as the city was built over a myriad of tunnels, and buildings have to respect weight restrictions.

416.

Annually, over three billion people take a passenger flight.

417.

Armpits have fewer sweat glands than feet.

418.

So far, no European country has won an Olympic title in women's table tennis.

419.

Sweden was the first European country to introduce banknotes.

420.

The state with the most confederate flags bought per capita is North Carolina, USA.

421.

Contrary to what sci-fi movies show, the average distance between asteroids is 1 million kilometres (600 000 miles).

422.

The aircraft, Solar Impulse 2, is equipped with 17 248 solar cells. Its cabin is not pressurised and, for reasons of economy, there is no heating.

423.

Cyprus intentionally sinks ships as part of its Artificial Reef Programme.

424.

The first ghetto was in Venice, nowadays Italy. 'Ghetto' meant 'foundry' in the Venetian dialect.

425.

Flipper machines contain 800 m (half a mile) of cables.

426.

'Black Swan' is the only Oscar-winning movie to be shot with a Canon 5D digital camera.

427.

Haribo gummy bears were marketed almost a century ago. 100 million of them are produced on any given day.

428.

In 1852, the first public flushing toilet opened in London, UK.

429.

The Internet allowed customers to swiftly compare insurance quotes. As a result, the prices of US life insurances fell dramatically in 1996.

430.

We slip on ice because there is always a tiny layer of liquid water on the top.

431.

It could be cheaper to buy a Greek island than a house in central London, UK.

432.

The mirror of the Hubble telescope had a tiny defect which became apparent only after it went into orbit.

433.

Mike Tyson once won a boxing match in just 5 seconds. The audience was outraged for having paid so much for such a short show.

434.

On average, the distance between stars is 35 trillion kilometres (22 trillion miles).

435.

There is almost no iron on the moon.

436.

A Romanian village spent €18 000 ($20 000) on a new football stadium, but decided to leave a huge tree in the middle of the pitch.

437.

In some cities, for example Madrid, Spain, and

Rome, Italy, the metro runs on left hand sided tracks.

438.

In the United Arab Emirates and Qatar, for every 100 women, there are more than 250 men.

439.

Caucasian smokers in the USA are more likely to buy Marlboro branded cigarettes than African American smokers.

440.

The term ‘green-on-blue attacks’ describes assaults on NATO forces by members of the Afghan security forces.

441.

Andy Warhol’s original name was Andrew Warhola. Both his parents were Slovak.

442.

Brazil has the greatest storage of fresh water worldwide.

443.

‘Pizza-Danish’ is the broken Danish language used by immigrants in the country.

444.

Budapest, Hungary, is home to Europe's largest synagogue.

445.

August 1985 witnessed more passenger and crew deaths on commercial airlines than any other month in history.

446.

Aspirin was named after *Spirea ulmaria* – the plant it was first extracted from.

447.

Jake and Molly are considered to be the 'whitest' American names. Imani and DeShawn are the 'blackest'.

448.

Turkish Airlines is the company that flies to the largest number of countries.

449.

Statistically, skyscraper builders have less fatal accidents when working without protective gear. Lack of protection makes them more alert and less accident prone.

450.

Gold medals are actually made of 93% silver, 6% copper and 1% gold.

451.

In 2008, the heavy metal group, Manowar, held its longest concert which lasted over five hours. The concert took place in Bulgaria.

452.

Some fancy restaurants don't allow you to photograph your food. Sorry, Instagram.

453.

A volcano can rise up from the ground at a speed of 200 m (650 feet) per week.

454.

The real name of the actor Kirk Douglas was Issur Danielovitch.

455.

South and North Korea are in different time zones.

456.

According to the rules of the International Olympic Committee, the host of the Winter Olympics could be a country without natural snow.

457.

During an earthquake, you are more likely to survive if you get under a table than if you stand in a doorway.

458.

Every minute, 30 000 minutes' worth of video are uploaded to YouTube (as of late 2015).

459.

Queen Elizabeth II has been reigning over the United Kingdom since 1952. She got her driver's licence before World War II and is still an active driver.

460.

Due to a typo, some editions of the King Charles' Bible preached: 'Thou shalt commit adultery'.

461.

Everyone in Iceland is obliged by law to learn how to swim.

462.

In Turkey, street vending machines accept plastic bottles and, in exchange, release food for homeless cats.

463.
There are six American flags on the moon.

464.
Helsinki, Finland, was built on 300 islands; Venice, Italy, on 100.

465.
Movie theatres are generally forbidden in Saudi Arabia. There is only one IMAX theatre in the country, located in Khobar.

466.
Honduras is the only volcano-free country in Central America.

467.
In Colombia, roasted ants are a popular snack.

468.
90% of the plants in New Zealand are not found anywhere else on Earth.

469.
Costa Rica did not issue a declaration of war against Germany in World War II as it had been technically still at war since World War I.

470.

In 2011, Samoa changed its time zone and, as a result, lost one day.

471.

Meteorites are not necessarily hot when they reach the ground.

472.

In 2015, the North Korean leader, Kim Jong Un, was nominated for an international peace prize.

473.

'123456' is the most common email password.

474.

Playboy magazine has a concealed bunny on each cover.

475.

A standard cup of brewed coffee contains more caffeine than a shot of espresso.

476.

The word 'Xmas' was first used in English 1000 years ago.

477.

In Sweden, an increasing number of companies have shortened the working day from 8 to 6 hours without changing the salary of employees. Overall productivity has remained unaffected.

478.

The torture devices named 'iron maiden' (see below) did not exist in medieval times. They were assembled as exhibition artefacts only 200 years ago.

479.

Today, there are up to 50 million uninhabited apartments in China, many of which are located in 'ghost' towns.

480.

Montenegro declared war on Japan in 1904. A peace treaty between the two countries was signed only in 2006.

481.

Hair care products cannot actually 'repair' split ends and damaged hair.

482.

Since 2014, there have been more mobile phones than TV sets worldwide.

483.

The French have a relatively low incidence of coronary heart disease, despite eating lots of saturated fats.

484.

Affordable methods of manipulating any kind of DNA at home already exist.

485.

Greenland is, in fact, much smaller than it appears on most maps.

486.

The ICD-10 Procedure Coding System is an international system of medical procedure codes. It contains crazy codes such as: 'V91.07XD: Burn due to water-skis on fire' or 'Z63.1: Problems in relationship with in-laws.'

487.

In New York City, USA, every Kuwaiti diplomat commits, on average, 246 driving violations per year. Not a single fine has ever been paid.

488.

Since 2009, the construction of mosque minarets in Switzerland has been outlawed.

489.

There are officially five rather than four tastes: sweet, salty, bitter, sour and umami.

490.

Bon Jovi's concerts are banned in China.

491.

Mangrove is the only tree that grows in saltwater.

492.

Some fake gold bars are hard to detect. They are made of gold-plated tungsten, which has a weight similar to that of gold.

493.

On Mount Everest, water boils at 71ºC (160ºF).

494.

The most popular car colours are: white in America, silver in Asia and black in Europe.

495.

Pluto had been predicted by Percival Lowell and when discovered after his death, was named after his initials. This was the same controversial guy who believed that Mars had man-made canals.

496.

Fidgeting burns up to 350 calories a day.

497.

Only two countries have used a single-coloured flag in recent years: from 1977 until 2011 the Libyan flag was plain green and from 1996 until 1997 the Taliban government in Afghanistan used a plain white flag.

498.

The pound sterling is the world's oldest continuously used currency. It has been in use since 1526.

499.

There is a hidden game in each Android device.

500.

RAP (as in rap music) stands for 'rhythm and poetry'.

501.

Denmark has the world's oldest continuously used flag. It has not been changed since the early 13th century.

502.

The car radio was first marketed in 1930.

503.

Bionic pants exist. They allow you to sit everywhere without a chair.

504.

The folding tables in airplanes are 10 times dirtier than the toilet lids in the same aircraft.

505.

Until 1980, Zimbabwe was called Rhodesia.

506.

The Spanish city of Tarragona uses DNA analysis in the fight against dog poop.

507.

Tallinn Airport, Estonia, makes security announcements in the form of a song.

508.

Women lose, on average, the equivalent of two days per year choosing what to wear.

509.

Ferruccio Lamborghini produced tractors before he decided he could make better cars than Ferrari.

510.

In late 2015, Playboy magazine announced that it would stop publishing photos of naked women.

511.

The frontiers of the solar system are not anywhere near the most distant planets. Going from the sun to the dwarf planet Pluto covers roughly 1/1000 of the entire distance.

512.

In Paris, France, there were plans to reuse some abandoned metro stations by converting them into public swimming pools.

513.

In 2014, while commenting on the murders of tourists, the Thai Prime Minister said that ‘only ugly women were safe wearing a bikini in Thailand’.

514.

Taller people are 70% more likely to get a job when competing against a shorter but similarly qualified candidate.

515.

In the period 1940-1956, the Soviet Union had a 16th republic, the Karelo-Finnish SSR.

516.

Recent studies have confirmed that boxing is almost twice as dangerous as MMA (Mixed Martial Arts) in terms of the risks of brain damage and retinal detachment.

517.

In 2015, an American bought the domain Google.com for $12. Due to a bug, the domain was put up for sale.

518.

In Georgia (a former republic of the Soviet Union), rugby is the second most popular sport as it strongly resembles an ancient local sport called ‘lelo burti’.

519.

In Chile, there are coins with a typo in circulation. They read ‘Chiie’ instead of Chile.

520.

The notorious terrorist, Ilich Ramírez Sánchez (a.k.a. Carlos the Jackal), was named after Lenin. His father had called his three sons Vladimir, Ilich and Lenin.

521.

The binding clip was invented in 1910.

522.

Studies show that a 10% increase in the price of cigarettes leads to a 4% drop in sales.

523.

The Lake Geneva fountain (Switzerland) sends water to an altitude of 100 m (330 feet). At any given moment, there are 8 tons of water in the air (see below).

524.

Lower-income and less-educated parents are more likely to dream of their children becoming professional athletes.

525.

For as long as five years, post-it notes were exclusively used by the manufacturer 3M's employees.

526.

70% of white sharks die in their first year.

527.

Netflix was initially called Kibble.com.

528.

87% of Americans have a Bible at home.

529.

Sound effects in movies use some bizarre yet ingenious techniques. The sound of steps in the snow is, for example, created by squeezing a bag of flour.

530.

Only 30% of people in India live in cities.

531.

Ukraine is the greatest exporter of sunflower seeds worldwide.

532.

Red LEDs last longer than blue ones.

533.

It is safe to refreeze raw meat, as long as it's not spoiled.

534.

A ton of recycled paper saves up to 18 trees.

535.

On average, we have four dreams every night.

536.

60% of CIA employees are private contractors.

537.

In Switzerland, there is a political party called the Anti-PowerPoint Party.

538.

The leaves of Amazon water lily can support up to 45 kg (100 pounds).

539.

The National Radio Quiet Zone is a large area of land in the USA (in West Virginia, Virginia, and Maryland states) in which radio transmissions are strictly restricted by law to facilitate scientific research and military intelligence.
Mobile phones and cars that run on petrol are prohibited.

540.

A study has proven that hearing only half of a conversation (for example, when a colleague talks on the phone) is more distracting than overhearing a normal conversation.

541.

Since 2007, around 45% of household savings in Europe have been in cash.

542.

To produce one beer, you need exactly 1 litre of water, 160 g of malt, 5 g of yeast and 2 g of hops.

543.

Camp Nou is the largest football stadium in Europe. It is located in Barcelona, Spain.

544.

The length of your foot is the same as that of your forearm between the wrist and the inside of your elbow.

545.

In space, astronauts cannot cry, as tears need gravity to flow.

546.

In a bizarre form of protest, a man sprayed three tons of liquid excrement in front of the headquarters of a political party in Moldova in 2015.

547.

Bono (the frontman of U2) makes more money from his investment in Facebook than from show business.

548.

Two of every three robots are in Japan.

549.

Colombia is the only country in South America that borders both the Caribbean Sea and the Pacific Ocean.

550.

Lamborghini models are often named after famous corrida bulls.

551.

In 2015, the highest peak in North America was renamed – from Mount McKinley to Denali.

552.

Barcelona, Spain, is amongst the most accessible cities for people in wheelchairs.

553.

On average, we spend two weeks of our life waiting at traffic lights.

554.

The plankton paradox: limited resources support an incredible number of plankton species.

555.

An early British toilet manufacturer produced a device called 'Waterloo' in honour of the Battle of Waterloo. The word was subsequently abbreviated to 'loo'.

556.

In 2015, the world's two biggest beer producers

announced a plan to merge in a $100 billion merger.

557.

In Slovakia, there is a football stadium through which trains regularly pass between the pitch and the tribunes. This even occurs during matches.

558.

In Bahrain, Qatar and the United Arab Emirates, there is no income tax.

559.

Spam food (gelatinous matter made of pork shoulder, ham, salt and potato starch) is considered a 'delicacy' in South Korea.

560.

Winston Churchill was the first honorary citizen of the USA.

561.

In ancient Babylon, they counted using 60 as a base (our decimal system has 10 as a base).

562.

Each Taser shot has a unique serial number, imprinted on tiny pieces of paper that scatter around when a shot is fired.

563.

Theoretically, you would need more than 1000 years to circumnavigate the largest known star in a jet travelling at 900 km/h (560 mph).

564.

It is complicated: green peppercorns are real peppercorns of *Piper nigrium* (originated in India).
Black peppercorns are simply cooked and dried green peppercorns.
White peppercorns are peeled black peppercorns.
Pink peppercorns are not peppercorns at all, but berries of the Brazilian pepper tree.

565.

The first meeting of the heads of state of West and East Germany took place in 1970, a full 25 years after the division of the country.

566.

An Indonesian volcano has electric-blue lava.

567.

The Lamborghini Countach was a really low car – only 1.07 m (42.1 inches) tall.

568.

Christmas, being an ancient pagan holiday, was illegal in the state of Oklahoma, USA, until 1907.

569.

'To the Struggle Against World Terrorism' is a 30 m (100 feet) sculpture that was given to the USA as an official gift by the Russian government on 11 September 2006. It stands in Bayonne, New Jersey.

570.

Several countries have already recognised the third gender and note it on official documents.

571.

To deliver a gift to every child in a single night, Santa needs his reindeer to fly 400 000 times faster than the speed of sound.

572.

Building the Hoover Dam on the Colorado River, USA, claimed the lives of 110 construction workers.

573.

In ancient Babylon, the groom drank an alcoholic beverage made of honey with his father-in-law exactly one month after the wedding, hence, the word 'honeymoon'.

574.

A church in Carey, Ohio (USA), houses an exact replica of the statue of 'Our Lady of Consolation', venerated in Luxembourg City's Cathedral.

575.

In the UK, every year, people bet on whether there will be snow on Christmas day.

576.

In 1999, the Swiss branches of UBS and Raiffeisenbank took a preventive measure against bank robberies. They decided not to admit clients in a Santa Claus outfit.

577.

Scientists could split the atom before they were able to calculate the age of Earth.

578.

Every year, there are, on average, 10 cases of plague in the USA.

579.

In the USA, ransom payments to kidnappers are tax-deductible.

580.

There is more cerium on Earth than copper.

581.

Tectonic plates move at the speed your nails grow.

582.

The Indian state railway company has more than one million employees.

583.

On average, two new coal power plants are built every week in China.

584.

Some particle accelerators only work at night. They consume so much electricity that during the day they would overload the grid.

585.

Italy borders the only two countries in the world with square flags: Vatican City and Switzerland (pictured on the next page).

586.

'Checkmate' literally means 'the king is dead'.

587.

Two dogs survived the sinking of the Titanic.

588.

In 1952, the smog in London, UK, killed some 12 000 people.

589.

In 1957, Malaysia was to become independent from Great Britain and held a global competition for a national anthem. Eventually, they rejected all 500 entries and chose a cabaret tune instead.

590.

On average, 100 people die in Russia in car accidents every day.

591.

Médecins Sans Frontières originated in response to the suffering in Biafra (a secessionist state in Nigeria, which existed between 1967 and 1970).

592.

The Greek national anthem has 158 lines. Many Greeks know it off by heart.

593.

The Caucasus Mountains have 12 peaks higher than the highest mountain in the Alps.

594.

According to a survey of 505 hiring managers, only 18% of them think that cover letters are an important part of the job application.

595.

In 1970, Betty Andrew ran as the Yippie's candidate for mayor of Vancouver, Canada. She promised to 'repeal every law, including the law of gravity so everyone can get high'.

596.

Twerking dance existed back in the 19th century.

597.

Machiavelli may have written 'The Prince' as satire. According to biographers, he was a strong opponent of all sorts of tyranny.

598.

CPR massages, performed to the rhythm of the song 'Staying Alive', are, in fact, very effective.

599.

Australia experiences droughts approximately every 18 years.

600.

23 June is the national holiday of Luxembourg, the official birthday of the Grand Duke. So far, none of the rulers was born on that date.

601.

Planning to invade Japan in 1945, the US military expected a blood bath and had 500 000 Purple Hearts readily ordered. With a stash so large, those same medals are still awarded today.

602.

In the 18th century, low quality salted beef or horse meat was called 'salt junk' or just 'junk'. It was actually the first 'junk food'.

603.

Andrew Jackson was called a 'jackass' by his opponents. He succeeded in turning that positive, by making the donkey the symbol of the US Democratic Party.

604.

In 1864, the elephant appeared as the US Republican symbol for the very first time in the pro-Lincoln newspaper 'Father Abraham'.

605.

South Korea carefully studied East Germany's integration into Germany. The conclusion: South Korea simply can't afford to integrate North Korea while preserving its current living standards.

606.

In early March 2015, ecstasy and meth became legal in Ireland for a day, due to a judicial error.

607.

Most people mistake London Bridge for Tower Bridge (both in London, UK).

608.

You may have an accent while speaking a foreign language. While singing however, your accent disappears.

609.

Blue roadside reflectors are used to keep wild animals away at night. Studies show that most animals associate blue light with danger as it is almost never seen in the wild.

610.

The can opener was invented exactly 48 years after the can itself.

611.

It is possible to grow watermelons in a square shape, a characteristic that greatly improves the efficiency with which they can be transported.

612.

In the 1940s, the failure to construct a weapon capable of destroying enemy airplanes from a distance actually resulted in the invention of radar.

613.

Almost 30% of all effective natural medicines were discovered in rainforests.

614.

Costa Rica has no army.

615.

There is a self-proclaimed independent country called the Republic of Lakotah within the USA. It is not yet recognised by any other country.

616.

The French habit of eating horse meat started in 1870 during the Franco-Prussian War.

617.

A big band normally has between 12 and 25 musical instruments.

618.

The suits on a deck of cards initially symbolised the following: hearts – the church; spades – the military; clubs – agriculture; and diamonds were dedicated to merchants.

619.

Sailors on the Mississippi river used to communicate the water depth by crying ‘Mark Twain’.

620.

James Fenimore Cooper's wife dared him to write a novel as she did not have anything good to read. Therefore, he wrote his famous novel 'Last of the Mohicans'.

621.

In Tokyo, Japan, the bicycle is a faster means of transport than the car.

622.

Catch-22 by Joseph Heller was supposed to be Catch-18.

623.

Each carriage of the Stockholm metro system has a unique name.

624.

Forgetting your wife's birthday is illegal in Samoa.

625.

Four of every five Dubai, UAE, residents are foreign born.

626.

The theorem of Pythagoras was known in Babylon centuries before Pythagoras formulated it.

627.

The pea is one of the oldest vegetables cultivated by humans.

628.

The last pocket to be introduced on Levi's jeans was the rear left one.

629.

The Iron Maiden song, 'The trooper', is dedicated to a real battle during the Crimean War, which was quite disastrous for the British.

630.

Campione d'Italia is Italy's only exclave in Switzerland. Exempt from VAT, it runs a casino just like in many Native American reservations.

631.

You could become a millionaire in US dollars by just using your math skills to prove Beal's conjecture.

632.

In the state of Iowa, USA, the law stipulates that a man with a moustache should not kiss a woman in public.

633.

Alzheimer's disease was described by many scientists before Alois Alzheimer.

634.

Laser nano-treatment of metals can make them truly hydrophobic.

635.

The Japanese word 'arigato' and Portuguese 'obrigado' both mean 'thank you' but are not related despite what many people think.

636.

The Streisand effect is the phenomenon by which the efforts to conceal a piece of information have the unintended consequence of publicising the information more widely (named after Barbara Streisand's attempt to suppress photographs of her house in Malibu, California (USA), which inadvertently drew further public attention to it).

637.

Luxembourg was declared a neutral state in 1867. One of the conditions was that Luxembourg City's fortress be torn down. The demolition works took 16 years.

638.

There was a piece of land, covering only 3.5 km^2 (1 square mile) between Germany and Belgium, which remained neutral for more than a century, until 1920.

639.

Fibonacci numbers were used in Indian mathematics 1500 years before Fibonacci was even born.

640.

Most baby carrots are mechanically cut out of bigger carrots.

641.

Bir Tawil is a 2000 km^2 (800 square mile) plot at the border between Egypt and Sudan, not yet claimed by either country.

642.

Mill Ends Park in Oregon, USA, is the smallest park in the world – 0.3 m^2 (451 square inches).

643.

All NATO AWACS airplanes in Europe are registered in Luxembourg.

644.

Nobody knows why the magnetic field of Earth shifts every 500 000 years.

645.

On average, airplanes fly 80% full, a much higher percentage than any other means of transportation.

646.

Romania's full official name (the long form) comprises just one word… Romania. The situation is the same for Hungary.

647.

Non-violent crime decreases as unemployment decreases.

648.

Jeff Atwood formulated a law: 'Any software that can be written in JavaScript will eventually be written in JavaScript'.

649.

The football player, Cristiano Ronaldo, has more than 110 million likes on Facebook.

650.

The brand BVLGARI was named after its founder Sotir Bulgari. His family name roughly translates as ‘Bulgarian’, even though he is Greek.

651.

There is a block of 960 flats in Moscow, Russia with a diameter of more than 200 m (700 feet), in the shape of a ring (see below).

652.

The Cyrillic alphabet was not invented by St. Cyril but by his disciples.

653.

Most Russian cars are equipped by their owners with a dashboard camera.

654.

Pluto is still considered a planet in the state of Illinois, USA.

655.

The F-111 fighter jet was equipped with ashtrays.

656.

The states of Hawaii and Arizona, USA, do not observe daylight saving time.

657.

There were no ponies in the Pony Express.

658.

There are 11 human body parts that are written with only 3 letters (jaw, rib, lip, eye, hip, arm, leg, ear, toe, gut and gum).

659.

Every third resident of Luxembourg is of Portuguese descent.

660.

During the Russo-Turkish War of 1877-78, a Japanese diplomat volunteered and fought the Turks in full Samurai uniform, armed only with a katana sword.

661.

In a weird competition in Finland, men carry their wives over a 220 m (700 feet) obstacle course. The top prize is the weight of the wife in beer.

662.

The Battle of Saragarhi (1897) was a heroic fight that lasted several hours between 21 Sikhs and 10 000 Afghan and Orakzai tribesmen.

663.

Pokemons were originally called Pocket Monsters.

664.

In the USA, a '13' in the address of a property will reduce its value by more than $5000.

665.

Maine is the only US state with a one-syllable name.

666.

Greece and Australia have not missed the Olympic Games since 1896.

667.

'Will Will Smith smith?' and 'Will Smith will smith.' are both sentences that make perfect sense.

668.

The hashtag symbol (#) is actually called an octothorp.

669.

The most expensive hole ever dug was in the state of Texas, USA. It cost over $2 billion and was part of a discontinued project called 'Superconducting Supercollider'.

670.

The first jack-o'-lantern was made from a hollowed out turnip.

671.

Soldiers from every country salute with their right hand.

CHAPTER 2

People and animals are awesome

1.
Injured fingernails grow faster than uninjured ones.

2.
Kangaroos cannot hop backwards. They cannot jump at all unless their tail is touching the ground.

3.
Catfish are the only animals that naturally have an odd number of whiskers.

4.
Koala fingerprints are not easily distinguishable from human ones.

5.
Honeybees have hair on their eyes.

6.
A turtle can breathe through its ass.

7.
Butterflies taste food with their feet.

8.
Horses cannot breathe through their mouth.

9.

More tigers live in the state of Texas, USA, than in the rest of the world.

10.

Most people cannot hum while holding their nose.

11.

The vast majority of readers have just tried to disprove the previous fact. ;)

12.

Rats and giraffes can survive longer than camels without water.

13.

Wombat's poop is square (see below).

14.

The fur of polar bears is not white but transparent.

15.

In 1968, a man escaped from East Germany to Denmark by literally riding a torpedo across the Baltic Sea.

16.

A chameleon's tongue is almost twice as long as its body.

17.

Dean Karnazes ran 50 marathons in all US states on 50 consecutive days.

18.

In China, a baby is considered to be 1 year old at birth.

19.

On 6 August 1945, 29-year-old Tsutomu Yamaguchi was in Hiroshima on business when the first A-bomb exploded. He arrived back home to Nagasaki to witness the second explosion and lived to the age of 93.

20.

All creatures but humans and captive chimpanzees look at the pointing finger and not in the direction it points.

21.

Koalas exclusively eat eucalyptus leaves. Such leaves contain cyanide and are lethal to most animals.

22.

In 1989, South Africa voluntarily dismantled its nuclear weapons.

23.

Coconut milk can substitute blood plasma for transfusion in emergency cases.

24.

When a species is considered extinct but then discovered to still be alive, it is classified as a member of the Lazarus species.

25.

The resolution of the human eye is estimated to be 576 megapixels.

26.

Most white cats with blue eyes are born deaf.

27.

The level of testosterone in our body determines the ratio between the length of the index finger and that of the ring finger.

28.

Goats, sheep and horses have rectangular-shaped pupils.

29.

By the time you turn 60, you will have lost half of your taste buds.

30.

There is enough carbon in your body to make 9500 pencils.

31.

Babies start to dream before birth.

32.

Most of the cells in your body are not of human origin. They are bacteria.

33.
The nail of the middle finger grows the fastest and the thumbnail - the slowest.

34.
Most sweat evaporates before you even notice it is there.

35.
Human hair is quite close to being indestructible.

36.
Consciousness can be retained for several seconds after decapitation.

37.
Long ago, our ancestors used to run after their prey until it died of exhaustion.

38.
Half of human DNA is identical to that of bananas.

39.
A human spermatozoon contains almost 40 Mb of DNA.

40.

Men suffer from hiccups more often than women.

41.

Humans are the only primates that shed emotional tears when crying.

42.

Rudolf, Santa's reindeer, must be a female reindeer. Male reindeer lose their antlers before Christmas, while females do not.

43.

A wrestler called Arrichion won the Ancient Olympic Games seconds after dying. With a broken neck and already dead, he was proclaimed the victor as his opponent had made the sign of submission and stopped the fight.

44.

Herrings use flatulence to communicate.

45.

Giraffes cannot drink water unless they spread their legs.

46.

When dying, Pancho Villa actually said: ‘Don’t let it end like this. Tell them I said something’.

47.

The majority of mammals, regardless of their size, need 21 seconds to urinate.

48.

Bird gender is determined by the chromosome pair ZW, in analogy to human XY.

49.

Agatha Christie started writing detective novels to win a bet with her sister.

50.

Mosquito repellents hide you from mosquito sensors.

51.

When in danger, wheel spiders roll away at over 30 rotations per second.

52.

Many Chinese women wear bathing suits that cover their face. Having a sun-tanned face has traditionally been associated with peasantry and is therefore undesirable.

53.

Castrated people generally live longer and are taller.

54.

Some fish species can accelerate as fast as a Porsche.

55.

In the state of California, USA, a blind architect continued working successfully after losing his sight in 2008.

56.

Birds use a V-shaped formation which improves efficiency for long flights by almost 70%. The first bird is rotated frequently to avoid fatigue.

57.

Muhammad Ali refused to join the army, saying publicly that 'no Vietcong ever called me nigger'.

58.

Fish do not grow new scales, but rather their scales increase in size. They can be used to reliably ascertain a fish's age.

59.

Horses prefer the taste of bananas to that of carrots.

60.

It was observed in many psychiatric institutions that those inmates with the same diagnosis had a propensity to establish strong friendships.

61.

New-born ladybugs are yellow.

62.

In 1964, Reg Spiers could not afford a flight ticket from London, UK, to Perth, Australia. Desperately looking for a cheaper alternative, he decided to send himself in a parcel. He survived this sixty-three-hour journey confined in a man-sized wooden box.

63.

Two handicapped Chinese men, one blind and the other armless, succeeded in planting 11 000 trees in the course of a decade.

64.

In 2002, Professor Kevin Warwick successfully connected his nervous system to a computer.

65.

As part of a social experiment, Maurizio Montalbini voluntarily spent seven months alone in a cave.

66.

Rick Allen, the drummer of Def Leppard, only has one hand and plays the drums just fine.

67.

Mahatma Gandhi wrote personally to Adolf Hitler, trying to dissuade him from starting World War II.

68.

Seals can be ginger.

69.

Colonel Sanders started KFC at the age of 65.

70.

Barry Marshall deliberately ingested bacteria that caused him stomach ulcers. This also led him to win the Nobel Prize.

71.

A ballerina has three times the pain threshold of the average woman.

72.

Studies suggest that humans are genetically programmed to fear spiders.

73.

Studies have shown that the Dutch are statistically the tallest nation in the world. The average height of Dutch men is 184 cm (6 feet).

74.

It is possible to acquire a food allergy after a blood transfusion.

75.

Kiwi eggs grow so big that they take up to one fifth of the mother's body (see below).

76.

There is an area in the Pacific Ocean called the 'White Shark Café', where a huge number of great white sharks get together. Nobody knows why.

77.

Multiple studies suggest that people with more body hair have higher intelligence.

78.

You do not necessarily die if you receive a transfusion of the wrong blood type.

79.

Pregnant women, suffering a heart attack or liver failure, can get stem cells from the foetus that repair the damaged organ.

80.

In desert regions, many animal species find their food in elephant dung.

81.

There are sound frequencies that most teenagers can hear but that are completely undetectable by adults.

82.

Most cows are made to swallow a magnet, which stays in their stomach for life, to prevent metal objects from entering their intestines.

83.

In 2013, on several occasions, it literally rained spiders in Brazil.

84.

Approximately 85% of what we perceive as 'taste' is actually due to our sense of smell.

85.

The Province of Flevoland, in the Netherlands, was reclaimed from the sea in the 1960s. Today, it is the largest artificial island in the world.

86.

To fill a 650 g (1.5 pound) jar of honey, a single bee needs to fly a distance greater than the length of the equator.

87.

In 2015, a Chinese company sent 6400 employees together on a vacation to France.

88.

The wood frog can freeze for several months, then thaw in the spring and jump away.

89.

Scorpions can live up to 13 months without food.

90.

Eagles can see in the ultraviolet spectrum and can detect the urine spots of their prey.

91.

There is a warm-blooded fish species called Opah (*Lampris guttatus*).

92.

In 2015, a woman got lost in a frosty forest in New Zealand and survived a couple of days by drinking her own breast milk.

93.

Women get 60% of tattoos.

94.

A Gurkha soldier lost his right hand during a World War II battle. He continued fighting, killing 31 enemy soldiers.

95.
Some crab species can regrow a leg.

96.
If women skip breakfast around the time of conception, it slightly increases their chances of having a girl.

97.
40 real squirrels were used while filming 'Charlie and the Chocolate Factory'. They were trained to sort nuts.

98.
The muscles of chimpanzees are four times stronger than those of humans.

99.
Bonobos were only discovered in 1929.

100.
The largest flying creature ever was not a bird but a lizard.

101.
Blood donors in Sweden receive a message whenever they have saved a life.

102.

Darwin frogs are not born or hatched, but are rather literally vomited out by their father.

103.

The sea mantis has the best eyes in terms of colour detection.

104.

Insects and mushrooms have something in common. Their cells are made up of chitin.

105.

Chimpanzees and gorillas only live north of the River Congo.

106.

The overwhelming majority of all 11 000 moss species are considered utterly useless from a business perspective.

107.

Jacob sheep have four to six horns.

108.

More people have visited the moon than the bottom of the Mariana Trench in the Pacific Ocean.

109.

Only four land species weigh more than a ton: elephants, hippopotamuses, rhinoceroses and giraffes.

110.

Optimistic people tend to be late for appointments more often.

111.

In 1999, Umberto Pelizzari dived unassisted to a depth of 150 m (492 feet) and survived.

112.

Each human cell contains 2 m (6.5 feet) of DNA.

113.

Albert Einstein started talking at the age of four.

114.

Leukocytes use oxygen to kill bacteria.

115.

Each morning you are taller than the night before and you can notice it. Some mornings, the rear view mirror in your car needs adjustment, right?

116.

In your body, purely statistically speaking, there are atoms that were part of Louis XIV's body.

117.

Adam Rainer (1899-1950) was both a dwarf and a giant in his lifetime. Aged 18, he was only 122.5 cm (4 ft. 0.25 in) tall; then, as a result of a pituitary tumour, he started growing and at the end of his life he had reached a height of 234 cm (7 ft. 8 in) (see below).

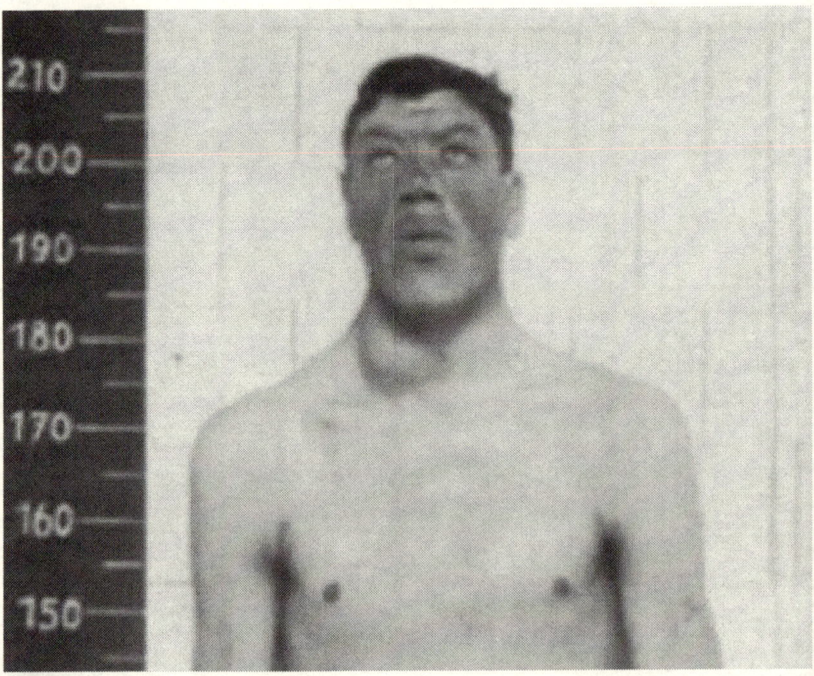

118.

The Sami people of Finland castrate reindeer with their teeth.

119.

The Founding Father, John Adams, defended British soldiers in court.

120.

Bill Gates saved Apple from bankruptcy on one occasion.

121.

Evolution has chosen weird locations for some lobster organs. Their brains are in their throats and their kidneys in their heads.

122.

The Masai people often steal food from lions.

123.

Elephants prefer rumba to tango.

124.

In 1985, Boris Becker won the Wimbledon singles title at the age of 17 years, 227 days. His record, as the youngest player to win the tournament, remains unbroken. In 1989, Michael Chang became the youngest male player to win the French Open at the age of 17 years, 110 days.

125.

At the cellular level, DNA is damaged and repaired more than 100 times a day.

126.

Plankton produces more oxygen than tropical forests.

127.

There are blonde Malaysian people who are not of European descent.

128.

Mitochondria, which we have in all our cells, behave like bacteria and have their own DNA.

129.

Male lions sleep roughly 20 hours a day.

130.

Only 1% of bacteria can be cultured in labs.

131.

Many people that commit suicide by jumping off a tall building actually die in mid-air from a heart attack.

132.

Apes have no tail.

133.

'Operation Cat Drop' refers to an instance in the 1950s, when the UK Royal Air Force delivered cats to a remote village in Borneo. The cats were dropped by parachute to combat a rat infestation.

134.

The teeth of Komodo dragons are very similar in shape to those of T-Rex.

135.

The smallest monkey is the pigmy marmoset. It is only 13 cm (5 inches) tall.

136.

Frogs never drink water with their mouth.

137.

75% of all animals on Madagascar are not found anywhere else on Earth.

138.

Usain Bolt runs 37 times faster than the fastest tortoise on Earth.

139.

Owls are the most silent birds when flying.

140.

Bees are very sensitive to magnetism.

141.

The platypus is the only venomous mammal and is one of only two that lay eggs.

142.

Snails have no sense of hearing.

143.

Pink flamingos are born white.

144.

The anablep fish has four eyes.

145.

Crocodiles eat on average 50 times a year.

146.

The closest relative to the Tasmanian devil is the kangaroo.

147.

The Latin word for 'walrus' means 'tooth-walking seahorse'.

148.

Chimerism is when a person has two sets of DNA.

149.

The kiwi is the only bird with nostrils at the tip of the beak.

150.

The smallest vertebrate is a frog, only 7 mm (1/4 inch) long (see below).

151.

The praying mantis is the only insect that can turn its head.

152.

Owls have asymmetric ears. They are not located where you think they are.

153.

The average adult can read 180 words per minute and has a vocabulary of about 6000 words.

154.

Hugging releases oxytocin, which helps to heal physical wounds.

155.

Reptile gender depends on the temperature at which their eggs hatch.

156.

A cat parasite has been proven to provoke mental illness in their owners.

157.

In many Asian countries, fish is thought to bring luck. This superstition was used by scientists who urged Cambodians to soak iron fishes in the food they cook. This has successfully eradicated anaemia in entire regions thanks to the increased iron intake.

158.

Rabbits can see their back without turning their head.

159.

Owls are the only birds that can see the colour blue.

160.

Hippopotamuses have such thick skin (5-6 cm or 2 inches) that most bullets simply cannot penetrate it.

161.

Thousands of prisoners serve as firemen battling wildfires in the state of California, USA. They do this dangerous job in exchange for early release.

162.

Millions of years ago, there were dragonflies with a wingspan of 65 cm (over 2 feet).

163.

Bruce Lee was also a great boxer. In 1958, he won the Hong Kong Boxing Championship by a knockout, of course.

164.

Bulls are colour-blind and do not hate red. They would react to the motion of whatever colour cloth you waved around.

165.

Dolphins do not need much sleep. Even when they do sleep, they close just one eye.

CHAPTER 3

Disturbing facts about our world

1.

In the United Kingdom, the most popular day for committing suicide is Monday.

2.

There are several confirmed cases of twins from different fathers.

3.

A chicken lived for over 18 months without a head. He was known as Mike the Headless Chicken (see below).

4.

In 2014, a barn in Germany exploded due to the ignition of the methane produced by 90 cows passing gas.

5.

Until 2005, juvenile offenders aged below 18 were still executed in the USA.

6.

Black people were exhibited in Brussels Zoo, Belgium, until the late 1950s.

7.

Giraffes are often electrocuted through contact with power lines. As a preventative measure, power lines are installed much higher in some African countries.

8.

In 2015, the Saudi government announced that it was hiring 8 executioners. They were to receive civil service employee benefits.

9.

In 1993, two British 10-year-old boys abducted, tortured and murdered a toddler. So far, they are the youngest convicted murderers in English history.

10.

In 2015, an Italian court obliged a vegan mother to feed her 12-year-old son meat as ‘the vegan diet was not healthy enough for minors’.

11.

In Canada, Native Indian and Inuit children were separated from their families and forced to attend special schools until 1998.

12.

In the USA, people with too high an IQ cannot become police officers.

13.

In 2014, the prime minister of New Zealand underwent medical tests to prove that he is not a reptile from space.

14.

In 2012, a drowsy Air Canada pilot saw a light and made a sharp manoeuvre to avoid a collision with what he thought was another airplane. He was actually avoiding the planet Venus.

15.

Male hippopotamuses defecate on younger male hippopotamuses to show who is higher up in the hierarchy.

16.

When interviewed by an Italian newspaper,

Pope Francis said that only 2% of the clergy are paedophiles.

17.

Worldwide, there are more male CEOs called John than there are female CEOs.

18.

In 2015, Amazon announced that they would not sell confederate flag merchandise any more. At the time of the announcement, they were still selling swastika items and Ku Klux Klan T-shirts.

19.

No women or female animals larger than a cat are allowed to go to Mount Athos, an autonomous monastic republic within Greece.

20.

Haiti and the USA were the only two countries in the world that abolished slavery through violence.

21.

In 1993, the Chilean trader, Juan Pablo Dávila, instructed his computer in error to 'buy' when he meant 'sell'. Within minutes, he singlehandedly wiped 0.5% off Chile's GDP.

22.

In 1996, representatives of the major US tobacco companies testified to Congress that 'nicotine is not addictive'.

23.

The Aral Sea was drained in just a few decades in one of the Soviet Union's crazy experiments.

24.

In 2006, a judge in the state of New Jersey, USA, approved the marriage of a 10-year-old boy and an 18-year-old woman.

25.

Llamas have a special pair of fighting teeth, used to bite off other llamas' testicles.

26.

During World War II, over 60 000 American citizens of Japanese descent spent time in internment camps on US soil.

27.

In 1933, Hitler passed a law for animal protection. In addition to stopping animal cruelty, it in practice outlawed kosher food.

28.

Atheists cannot hold public office in some US states.

29.

In the Battle of Karansebes, Austrian troops fought each other by mistake, killing and wounding 10 000 soldiers.

30.

Since 2000, interracial marriages have no longer been a crime in the state of Alabama, USA.

31.

In India, children are paid to use a toilet as part of a social project that aims to instil basic toilet habits.

32.

More Americans died from gun related violence in the last 60 years in times of peace than on the battlefields of all wars in American history combined.

33.

In 2015, a Google algorithm tagged pictures of African Americans as 'gorillas'. The company apologised.

34.

A disproportionately large number of the USA's most notorious serial killers were born in the month of November.

35.

The Candiru fish in the Amazon River would try to enter through your urethra if you urinated in the water.

36.

In 2015, timber cutter was the most dangerous job in the USA.

37.

In the Middle Ages, grave robbing and body snatching was not criminalised in England.

38.

In 1930, a US prison inmate used a deck of cards to create an improvised explosive device. He used it to successfully commit suicide.

39.

The first car accident with casualties occurred in London, UK, in 1896. An English lady was run over by a car, travelling at 15 km/h (9 mph).

40.

Owls prefer catching pregnant mice.

41.

US President John F. Kennedy bought 1200 Cuban cigars hours before he authorised the Cuban embargo.

42.

Seagulls sometimes attack baby seals and eat their eyeballs.

43.

Heroin was first marketed by the German pharmaceutical corporation Bayer and was initially sold over the counter (see below).

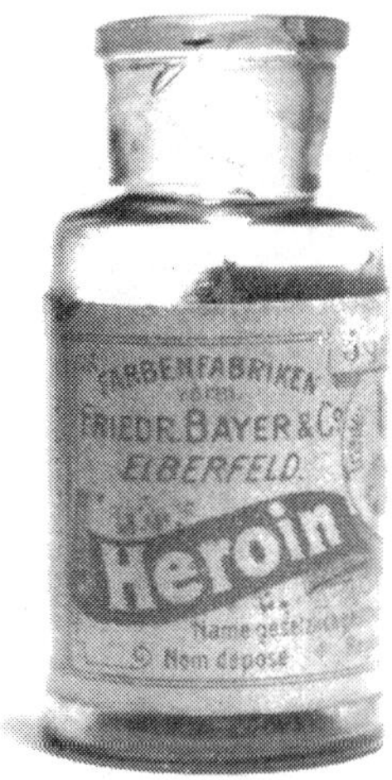

44.

The 46th Vice President of the United States, Dick Cheney, shot a man in the face and the victim apologised.

45.

In the 1940s, American soldiers saved the life of the future president of Vietnam, Ho Chi Minh.

46.

After the end of the Nazi occupation, French mobs shaved the heads of over 20 000 women, all of whom were accused of having had affairs with German soldiers.

47.

The US Drug Enforcement Administration can seize your money without a court decision, without even pressing charges.

48.

The island of Saint Helena lost all of its forests as a result of the introduction of goats by the British.

49.

Drug dealers in Chicago have a statistically higher chance of dying than prisoners on death row.

50.

Some extravagant and rich people buy capsules of pure gold dust that, when ingested, make their stool glitter.

51.

Martin Luther King's family sued the US government for conspiracy to commit murder and won.

52.

Thomas Midgley Jr. is the man who has caused the greatest damage to our planet. He invented both the lead add-on for fuel and CFC (Freon).

53.

No death by spider has been reported in Australia since 1979.

54.

'Montezuma's revenge' is a Mexican colloquial term for traveller's diarrhoea, contracted by foreign tourists.

55.

More than 99.9% of all species that ever inhabited Earth are now extinct.

56.

In 1918, US prisoners volunteered for a Spanish flu vaccine experiment, in which the survivors were to be pardoned. The only casualty was the doctor.

57.

In 2015, Australia declared war on cats, planning to kill two million of them in the course of the following five years.

58.

The Belgian King, Leopold II, encouraged the practice of 'severed hands' in Belgian Congo in order to increase rubber production. Mercenaries and soldiers were encouraged not to waste bullets while terrorising the population and were paid bonuses on the basis of how many hands they collected.

59.

The Cobra effect manifests when an attempted solution to a problem makes the problem worse. The government in colonial India at one time offered a reward for every dead cobra in a bid to decimate the poisonous snake population in Delhi. Some people, however, began to breed cobras for profit and the cobra population skyrocketed.

60.

Molotov cocktails were named after an actual Soviet minister of foreign affairs. In 1939, when the USSR treacherously invaded Finland, the Finns came up with improvised anti-tank incendiary weapons, which were bottle-based.

61.

Cone snails use insulin as a weapon.

62.

On average, real estate agents sell their own properties at a 4% higher price than the properties that they sell for clients, keeping them on the market for longer.

63.

Sea slugs are capable of stealing photosynthesis genes from algae and undergoing photosynthesis themselves.

64.

So far, bird flu, a.k.a. avian influenza, has killed a total of 400 people worldwide. The common flu, however, claims millions of lives each year.

65.

Low-cost air carriers explored the option of removing some of the seats in the aircraft, thus offering even cheaper standing tickets for passengers.

66.

In the early 1900s, horses polluted cities with tons of dung and automobiles were seen as a green alternative.

67.

There are studies linking lower IQ with xenophobia.

68.

In 1932, the Australian Army waged the Great Emu War, using regular troops and machine guns to cull emus.

69.

When Margaret Thatcher died, the song 'Ding Dong! The Witch is Dead' reached number 2 in the British charts.

70.

Mauritania only officially outlawed slavery in 2007.

71.

In 2012, a unit of elite French commandos undertook unauthorised training drills in the Bulgarian countryside. They were attacked and beaten up by angry local peasants who mistook them for thieves.

72.

The marketing department of the store Target (USA) predicted that a teenage girl was pregnant just by analysing her shopping history. At the time, Target sent her personalised brochures for baby merchandise thus alerting her parents, who up until that point were unaware of the pregnancy.

73.

Environmental organisations insist that palm oil production (an ingredient of Nutella) has decimated the orang-utan population of Borneo.

74.

In 1992, members of the French scouting organisation damaged prehistoric paintings, naively thinking that they were removing graffiti.

75.

In North Korea, anyone reading the Bible or watching porn could face the death penalty.

76.

Iranian men who do not marry stay with their birth family all their life and are called 'na-mard' (not-men).

77.

Mr. Forrest Fenn claims to have hidden a treasure worth over $1 million in the Rocky Mountains, USA. He wrote a poem purportedly containing all the clues needed to discover it.

78.

In Germany, the lower part of the walls of some buildings is covered with a super hydrophobic substance that splashes back pee if the wall is used as a urinal.

79.

Rachel Dolezal, spokesperson of the US National Association for the Advancement of Coloured People, pretended to be black, although she is actually Caucasian (see photo). Ironically, she had once called for a boycott of the movie 'Exodus: Gods and Kings' for casting white actors as Africans.

80.

In the period 1991-92, Colombia was the world's most dangerous place, with an estimated total of 55 000 violent deaths.

81.

Historically, rich British people would allow poor people to live in their newly built house for free, until the humidity from the walls disappeared.

82.

Divorce is illegal in Vatican City and the Philippines.

83.

Over the last century, humans have killed more than three million whales.

84.

In 1980, Las Vegas hospital workers (USA) were fired for betting on which patient would die next.

85.

In 2001, the US Financial Accounting Standards Board did not qualify 9/11 as 'an extraordinary event' for accounting purposes.

86.

In 2015, a woman called Kam Brock was forcibly admitted to a psychiatric hospital in New York City, USA, and kept for 8 days after mentioning that President Obama followed her on Twitter. She was not lying.

87.

The last public execution in the USA took place in 1936.

88.

Statistically, more African Americans are killed by police officers than by terrorists.

89.

Most serial killers have personality disorders, such as paranoia, excessive rage, delusions of grandeur and not serious mental illnesses like schizophrenia.

90.

A couple of years ago, Tibetan mastiffs cost $200 000 in China. Now the fad is over and they cost as little as $5 and are often eaten.

91.

In Ferguson, Montana (USA), partly due to the higher imprisonment rates of African Americans, for every 100 black women aged between 25 and 54, there are only 60 black men.

92.

Moths can imitate bees' scent and can enter unnoticed into a hive.

93.

The great majority of Tasmanian devils suffer from a deadly face cancer.

94.

Israel and the USA do not recognise the 'Armenian genocide' of 1916.

95.

In China, there used to be a smartphone app for hiring mobsters online to beat somebody up.

96.

Real estate agents in China often hire white people to inhabit certain buildings in order to give the place an 'international' look and hopefully raise the price.

97.

The fake medicine business is 15 times more profitable than selling heroin.

98.

The so-called 'Horror Frog' can break its toe bones, force the broken ends through its skin and, thus, create claws.

99.

Some Australian spiders eat lizards and snakes (see photo).

100.

The homicide rate in New Orleans is 10 times the US average. If it were an independent country, it would rank in the top three most dangerous countries worldwide.

101.

There are pig farms in China in which pigs are forced to jump from over 10 m (35 feet) into water as an attraction for tourists.

102.

One international border is easily recognisable on satellite images. As Haiti cut down virtually all of its trees, the Dominican Republic looks much greener.

103.

The world's shortest skyscraper is located in Wichita Falls, Texas (USA). It was expected to be 150 m (480 feet) but ended up being only 12 m (480 inches) tall as the developer cheated.

104.

In 2002, an informant in the state of Texas, USA, used to plant chalk powder in the cars of random Mexicans. He would then inform the police and receive hundreds of thousands of dollars in reward. It was not until after six months of this charade that the police suspected foul play.

105.

Swaziland's authorities blamed miniskirts for spreading AIDS.

106.

Until 2009, many teachers in the state of California, USA, were given $25 000 for exceptional results. The bonuses were eventually revoked, as much of the money was found to be going to teachers who had helped their students to cheat.

107.

80% of contraband reptiles worldwide are smuggled into the USA.

108.

In the USA, for every person killed in self-defence, 35 innocent people die.

109.

Nazi scientists did not take Jewish physicists seriously enough. It was one of the main reasons why Germany lagged behind in the development of nuclear weapons.

110.

0.7% of the world's population are either refugees or people displaced against their will.

111.

China has a history of numerous meat scams. Some entrepreneurs sell rat and fox meat labelled as 'lamb' or 'chicken'.

112.

In 1963, American Express and Bank of America lost over $1 billion (adjusted for inflation) giving loans that were secured with water disguised as salad oil.

113.

In 1921, the US army assaulted participants in a coal miners' strike with machine guns and planes.

114.

Asbestos was used as fake snow until the 1960s.

115.

Overtoun Bridge, near Dumbarton, Scotland, is shrouded in mystery. 50 dogs in the last 50 years have jumped to their death from that bridge for unknown reasons.

116.

A Hungarian World War II prisoner-of-war was held for 53 years in the Soviet Union. He returned home in the 1990s.

117.

In South Korea, mixed-race Koreans were banned from serving in the army until 2006.

118.

In the USA, rattlesnakes are responsible for three out of every four snake bites.

119.

Until the 19th century, people thought that stones slowly turn into living creatures. They were observing lichens.

120.

In Japan, more criminal acts are committed by people over the age of 65 than by teenagers.

121.

Charles Darwin played the piano to worms as part of an experiment.

122.

Mites living on your skin breed faster if you wash your clothes at lower temperature.

123.

Some countries did not screen the movie 'E.T.' as it depicted adults as the enemies of children.

124.

Astroturfing is the unethical PR practice of masking the real sponsors of a message, making it appear as though it comes from grassroots participants.

125.

The sloth is the only animal named after a sin.

126.

Radioactive consumer goods were manufactured until 1938.

127.

At altitudes higher than 5500 m (18 000 feet), there is not enough oxygen for a healthy baby to be born.

128.

Lead-containing paint was prohibited in Europe in the 1950s. It continued to be used in the USA until the 1990s.

129.

For every ton of shrimps caught, 8 tons of other sea creatures are killed as collateral damage.

130.

In the 1950s, some pregnancy tests involved injecting women's urine into the skin of male frogs.

131.

Hugo Boss designed the uniforms of the notorious SS troops.

132.

The first nuclear waste was simply dumped by the USA and the Soviet Union into the oceans in plain metal containers. If the containers did not sink, the navy would shoot at them to make them take in water.

133.

When a traveling Ku Klux Klan member wanted to find fellows in a new town, he would ask for a 'Mr. Ayak'. 'Ayak' stood for 'Are you a Klansman?'

134.

In 2010, a US teacher faked her child's death to extend a vacation in Costa Rica.

135.

When astronomer Edwin Hubble died in 1953, his wife refused to organise a funeral. To this day, nobody knows what happened to his body.

136.

A bachelor tax was enforced in several socialist states until the early 1990s.

137.

People are more inclined to give money to a beggar claiming he needs the money to buy weed, rather than to one who claims he needs it to support his family.

138.

The inventor of the Geiger counter, Hans Geiger, became an ardent Nazi supporter and reportedly facilitated sending several fellow scientists to concentration camps.

139.

In 1988, one in four homicides in New York City, USA, was crack related.

140.

Many more US infants die drowning in swimming pools than playing with weapons.

141.

Mary E. Surratt, a participant in the conspiracy to assassinate President Abraham Lincoln, was the first woman to be executed by the US federal government.

142.

Approximately 400 bee stings will kill an adult human being.

143.

In 2015, a Louisiana man asked a US Walmart store to bake him a cake with the confederate flag on it. The store refused. Ironically, it later baked one with the Islamic State battle flag instead.

144.

In July 2015, the UK police was informed of a car accident. It took them three full days to respond. Luckily, the severely injured woman who was trapped in the car survived.

145.

A quarter of people shot dead by the US police showed signs of mental illness.

146.

In the state of Massachusetts, USA, a 36-year-old woman drowned in a busy swimming pool with six lifeguards on duty. Nobody noticed her floating body for two full days.

147.

In France, a pill is available that supposedly makes your farts smell like roses and chocolate.

148.

Pepsi were once offered Coca Cola's secret recipe on the black market. Rather than purchasing it, however, they alerted the FBI.

149.

While covering a story on a gay parade, the news agency CNN mistook a banner depicting dildos for the ISIS flag (see below).

150.

Worldwide, more people have cell phones than access to toilets.

151.

More money is spent on studies on how to neuter your pet than on the development of a human male contraceptive pill.

152.

In the USA, there are currently more overweight people than people with a healthy body weight.

153.

In 1941, the criminal, Robert Phillips, had skin from his abdomen transplanted to his fingertips. It is purportedly the only successful case in history of permanently erasing one's fingerprints.

154.

China recently started a harsh anti-corruption campaign. As a result, the income of Macao's casinos has dropped by 60%.

155.

When the city of Atlanta, USA, was preparing for the 1996 Olympic Games, the police reported only some crimes so that the city appeared safer.

156.

The Ku Klux Klan's bible was called the Kloran.

157.

If your body cools down by only 2°C, you will start to experience hypothermia.

158.

Studies have shown that men put on weight when they become parents.

159.

Average life expectancy in the 18th century was slightly below 30. This was, in large part, due to the extremely high rate of infant mortality.

160.

1/8 of the world's population is undernourished.

161.

Humans are one of the smelliest mammals. Luckily, most of us take frequent showers.

162.

An innocent man, Glenn Ford from Louisiana, USA, spent 30 years on death row. After his release, as compensation, he received $20 for a bus ride home from prison.

163.

An Austrian man intentionally severed his foot to collect unemployment benefit. The state refused and instead offered him a job suitable for handicapped people.

164.

Tasmanian devils sometimes sleep inside their prey.

165.

Babies with a low birth weight will statistically perform worse in school than those born with a normal weight.

166.

Statistically, obese people have less than a 10% chance of returning back to and maintaining a healthy weight.

167.

In the USA, the census value of a slave used to be 60% of the value of a free person. After the abolition of slavery, the former slaves continued to be counted using this value for some time.

168.

Some bacteria can survive in sulphuric acid and in the cooling water of nuclear reactors. What's more, they can reproduce in such inhospitable conditions, dividing every 9 minutes.

169.

On average, it takes four million years for a complex animal species to become extinct.

170.

Ozzy Osbourne has indicated that he wishes to have his body donated to science when he dies, saying: 'it's a medical miracle I'm still alive after years of endless partying'.

171.

In the USA, the most deadly animal, statistically, is human kind.

172.

In 2004, Californian politician, Richard Riordan, told a 6-year-old girl that her name Isis meant 'stupid girl'. US black activists demanded his resignation, chanting day after day 'Would he say that to a white girl?' Ironically, it turned out that Isis was a white girl. Richard Riordan remained in office.

173.

In 2015, a pigeon was caught trafficking cocaine into a Costa Rican prison.

174.

Today, there are more sculptures of lions than real lions.

175.

Lemmings, in fact, do not commit suicide by jumping off cliffs. A Disney documentary movie is responsible for propagating this myth.

176.

Each year, police chases in the USA kill more people than floods, tornadoes, hurricanes and lightnings combined.

177.

In September 2015, all the delegates of a German homeopathy conference took a hallucinogenic drug. Havoc ensued.

178.

In 2015, a man was sentenced, by a judge in the state of Texas, USA, to marry his 19-year-old girlfriend.

179.

There are more than 5000 jails and prisons in the USA.

180.

The ancient Mayans took hallucinogenic drugs through their rectums.

181.

In the 1920s, Rockwell Sayre from Chicago, USA, tried to kill as many cats as possible. He also rewarded followers by paying 10 cents for each cat corpse.

182.

In 2009, a former Montreal stripper convinced the Canadian tax court that a $2 million tip from a client was a gift and, thus, exempt from tax.

183.

Pepsi stated officially that a mouse would be completely dissolved if soaked in the soft drink Mountain Dew for a month.

184.

Half of all polar bear cubs die in their first year.

185.

A giant Japanese hornet can kill up to 40 bees in a single minute.

186.

A US neuroscientist was checking the brain scans of murderers, comparing their empathy zone with that of normal people. He found one of the scans from the 'normal' pile to be like those of the psychopaths. To his great surprise, it turned out to be his own brain scan.

187.

In Saudi Arabia, only men drive. Yet, car accidents are amongst the leading causes of death.

188.

Serial bombers have the highest IQ amongst all serial killers.

189.

Los Angeles International Airport, USA, once tried to ban all First Amendment activities, such as the freedom to exercise religious practices and freedom of speech, within its perimeter.

190.

During the Cold War, Stalin's daughter defected to the USA.

191.

In 2014, a white woman was accidentally impregnated with a black man's sperm by the US Midwest Sperm Bank. She sued and lost.

192.

In Vatican City, women do not have the right to vote.

193.

Historically, in many prisons worldwide, inmates communicated using a tapped alphabet, similar to Morse code.

194.

The 17th congress of the Communist Party in the Soviet Union was dubbed the 'Congress of the Condemned' as most of its delegates were sentenced to death in the course of the next year.

195.

In the period 1936-39, every second Red Army general was executed by Stalin.

196.

In several countries, women are not required by law to wear helmets while riding a motorcycle.

197.

Air pollution kills more people than malaria and HIV/AIDS combined.

198.

'The Crusader' is a US assault rifle designed especially for Christians. It costs about €1200 ($1400) and has a safety selector with options: 'Peace' for safe, 'War' for semi-automatic, and 'God wills it' for full automatic mode.

199.

R The crash of the inter-planetary probe, Mariner 1, cost $80 million. It was due to a forgotten overbar (a horizontal line written above a mathematical symbol) over the letter 'R' in one of the formulas that went unnoticed and messed up the orbit calculations.

200.

Since 1960, the world has spent more money on arms each decade than all of the military expenses during the two world wars combined.

201.

A recent study suggests that people who like bitter-tasting foods have a higher chance of developing sadistic traits.

202.

'Artist's Shit' is a 1961 artwork by the Italian artist, Piero Manzoni. It comprises 90 tin cans, each containing 30 g (1.1 ounces) of faeces.

203.

American households possess more exotic animals than American zoos.

204.

In US counties in which alcohol is outlawed, there is, on average, a higher rate of meth-related crime.

205.

Volkswagen integrated a cheating device into millions of cars to tamper with emission tests.

206.

The more stickers on the bumper, the higher the probability that the respective driver is prone to violence.

207.

Half of the 12 deadliest shootings in the history of the USA happened after 2007.

208.

Millions of Chinese people still live in caves.

209.

In 2005, the citizens of Hamburg, Germany, witnessed a strange incident. In city parks and ponds, thousands of frogs began bloating and spontaneously bursting into pieces.

210.

In Peru, guinea pigs are raised extensively for food.

211.

95% of Americans are not allowed by law to invest in start-ups. Only 'accredited investors' are entitled to do so.

212.

In 2009, a bat took a free ride to space, clinging onto a NASA shuttle as it launched.

213.

Adele Penguins defecate explosively, ejecting poop up to half a meter (1.5 feet) from their bodies. This distance is almost equal to their height.

214.

Male visitors with long hair were not admitted to Disneyland until the late 1960s.

215.

In 1958, exactly 10 years before his assassination, Dr. Martin Luther King was stabbed in the chest.

216.

Cows are deadlier than sharks.

217.

More Russians (both civilians and military personnel) died during the siege of Leningrad alone than all British and American casualties combined (including civilians) during the whole of World War II.

CHAPTER 4

Facts about human and animal sexuality

1.

Lisa Sparks, USA, holds the record for the largest number of sex partners in a single day, after having slept with 919 men in less than 24 hours.

2.

NASA renamed the sizes of early condom-based space toilets from ‘small, medium and large’ to ‘large, gigantic and humongous’ because the ego of male astronauts led them to take ‘L’ regardless of their real size.

3.

Male coin spiders tear off their own genitalia after sex.

4.

In most US states, being fired for your sexual orientation is not yet outlawed.

5.

Corn Flakes were invented as part of Kellogg’s health regimen to prevent masturbation.

6.

Anacondas mate in a curious way. Up to 12 males have an orgy with just one female. The ritual can last up to two days.

7.

At any given moment, some 32 million people are watching porn.

8.

Norway plans to lower the legal age for sex change operations to 7.

9.

Carolus Linnaeus categorised species in the 18th century. Obsessed by sexuality, he named a plant Clitoria and described the body parts of a seashell as 'vulva, labia, pubes, anus and hymen'.

10.

In the US military, it is possible to be court-martialled for adultery.
The maximum punishment is dishonourable discharge and confinement for up to 1 year.

11.

There is a shortage of male porn actors in Japan. Whilst there are about 11 000 actresses, there are only 68 male actors.

12.

In 2015, a Brazilian woman called Ana Catarian Bezerra was allowed by a court to watch porn and masturbate at work.

13.

Bats practise oral sex.

14.

The South Park: Bigger, Longer & Uncut cartoon featured a real picture of an erected penis, disguised as a sex toy. Surprisingly, it was not rated 'for adults only'.

15.

Samurai warriors often had same-sex lovers while on a military campaign.

16.

Sea otters have such violent sex that it leads to numerous female deaths.

17.

Male koalas have two penises. Luckily, females have two vaginas.

18.

No NC-17 rated film (for adults over the age of 17 due to explicit sexual or violent content) has ever made $25 million at the box office.

19.

There are several documented cases of a woman getting pregnant while she was already pregnant.

20.

Male dolphins are known to gang-rape females.

21.

Many mammals have a baculum (a bone inside their penis, see below).

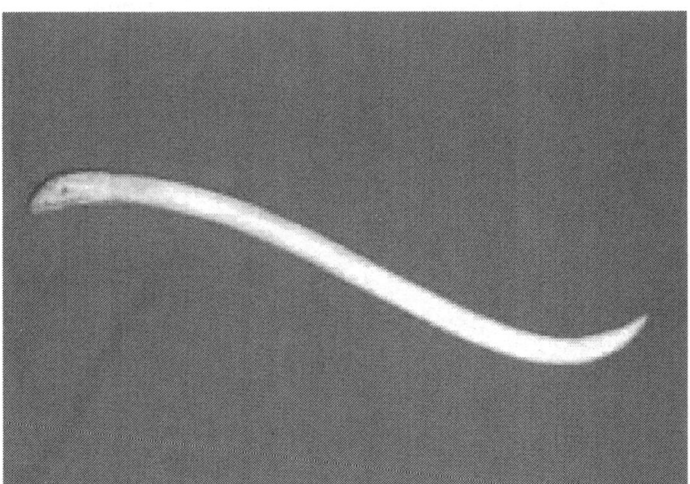

22.

Men's bodies contain more water than women's. The opposite is true in the case of pregnancy.

23.

In China, some pregnancy tests are sold together with a discount coupon for an abortion clinic.

24.

The Dutch government pays for lap-dances and prostitutes for disabled people.

25.

Across most cultures, women seek ambitious and high-earning men. Men mostly look for attractive women.

26.

Redheads are turned down as semen donors in Denmark.

27.

Swans, albatrosses, bald eagles, penguins and beavers are all monogamous.

28.

'Transmission of Gonorrhoea through an Inflatable Doll' is the name of a real medical report.

29.

Many pregnant animals have symptoms similar to those experienced by pregnant women.

30.

It is estimated that one third of all Internet traffic is generated by porn.

31.

There is no minimum age foreseen by law for marriage in Saudi Arabia.

32.

In San Francisco, California (USA), 6.7% of the residents are gay.

33.

A dildo, holding exactly 21 g (0.74 ounces) of the cremated ashes of your deceased partner, is already being marketed.

34.

The adult website, Pornhub, plans to shoot a porn movie in space.

35.

What do Sylvester Stallone and Jackie Chan have in common? They both starred in softcore porn movies.

36.

As you might expect, Christmas is the least popular day for watching porn online.

37.

In a weird TV show in Japan, men compete at singing while being jerked off by a female show assistant.

38.

On online dating websites, both genders receive five times fewer replies if their profile has no picture.

39.

Statistically speaking, an architect is much more likely to hire a prostitute than the other way round.

40.

There was a time when Whitehouse.com was a porn site.

41.

Male kangaroos flex their biceps to impress females.

42.

In web dating, it is a handicap for men to be bald, have ginger hair or be in a low-income job. Women lose points for being overweight or having salt and pepper hair.

CHAPTER 5

You have been warned - don't try this at home!

1.

If a cat falls from the 7th floor of a building, it has less chance of surviving than if it falls from the 20th floor.

2.

It's not that easy to set a large quantity of diesel on fire. At room temperature, a single match will not ignite 4 litres (a gallon) of diesel in a bucket.

3.

There are registered deaths caused by drinking too much carrot juice.

4.

The most painful place to be stung by a bee is the inside of the nostril.

5.

If a tornado comes your way and you have no better shelter, a relatively safe position is to lie flat in a ditch.

6.

In 1972, the Yugoslavian stewardess Vesna Vulovic fell without a parachute from a height of over 10 km (33 000 feet) when her plane exploded. She survived.

7.

In 1994, spilt coffee scalded the lap of an elderly woman at a McDonald's parking lot in the state of New Mexico, USA. The company had to pay her damages of $2.8 million.

8.

In 2015, a 22-month-old child was revived 2 hours after drowning in freezing water in Buffalo Creek, Pennsylvania (USA).

9.

In 1954, Captain John Paul Stapp, a US medical doctor and scientist, voluntarily experienced deceleration exceeding 40G and survived.

10.

A Russian man has volunteered for the first human head transplant. The operation is planned for December 2017.

11.

In 1991, Petty Officer J.D. Bridges was sucked into a working jet engine and survived.

12.

You are six times more likely to die climbing Mount Annapurna, Himalayas, than Mount Everest.

13.

In 1980, a two-month warning was given about the eruption of Mount St. Helens, USA, but it still claimed 57 lives. Most of the victims were tourists who deliberately came to witness the eruption.

14.

Many US skyscrapers, towers and bridges were built by fearless ironworkers from the Mohawk tribe, a.k.a. Indian Skywalkers.

15.

In medieval Germany, there was a crazy invention called the Katzenklavier (cat piano). Cats had their tails fixed to a keyboard and cried out in pain when a key was pressed to pull the cat's tail (see below).

16.

If you inhale black mould, it starts growing in your lungs and will eventually kill you.

17.

In 2009, a breast implant saved a woman's life in the USA when she was shot at point blank range with an AK-47 assault rifle.

18.

A Brooklyn restaurant (USA) offers a 10% ownership stake if you eat their 'Gran Chingon' burrito in one sitting. It weighs 13.6 kg (30 pounds).

19.

To mark the end of summer training at the West Point Military Academy, USA, cadets organise a massive pillow fight. In 2015, over 30 people were injured.

20.

No one has ever been killed by a champagne cork. Many have, however, been blinded.

21.

Drinking over 6 lit. (1.5 gallons) of water can kill you.

22.

In 2015, a Norwegian study found that a vitamin A overdose may increase the risk of lung cancer in both smokers and non-smokers.

23.

At full speed, a train would need up to 1.6 km (almost a mile) to come to a complete halt. If the train driver can see you before braking, it is already too late.

24.

After every knockout suffered, boxers are supposed to take a break of 45 days before the next game.

25.

Since it opened in 1937, some 1600 people have committed suicide by jumping from the Golden Gate Bridge, USA.

26.

In the USA, vending machines kill more people than sharks do.

27.

In 2014, more people died while trying to take a selfie than in shark-related accidents.

28.

In 2011, a woman survived a grenade attack in Mexico. The grenade got stuck on her face without exploding and had to be removed by surgeons and sappers.

CHAPTER 6

Debunked myths or unsubstantiated urban legends

1.

The elephant is the only animal with four knees. *(false – technically, it has two knees)*

2.

The moon is not the only natural satellite of Earth. *(false – no other object has stayed in orbit long enough to be considered a satellite)*

3.

Donald Duck was banned in Finland for not wearing trousers. *(false)*

4.

Kangaroos never fart. *(false)*

5.

So far, nobody has succeeded in eating a spoonful of ground cinnamon for less than a minute without drinking any water. *(false – don't try it, however!)*

6.

Polar bears are left-handed. *(not proven)*

7.

'GOLF' means 'Gentlemen Only Ladies Forbidden'. *(false)*

8.

In France, you cannot call a pig Napoleon. *(false)*

9.

Only a few rivers in the world flow north. *(inaccurate – plenty of rivers do)*

10.

Sex toys are prohibited in India. *(false)*

11.

Crime in New York City dropped significantly as a result of measures such as fixing broken windows, painting over graffiti and arresting free riders in the metro. *(not proven – many instead attribute it to the birth-control pill, introduced exactly 18 years prior to the observed drop in crime. It apparently removed many 'unwanted' children from the streets, who normally would have joined gangs.)*

12.

Crocodiles are the only reptiles that take care of their offspring. *(inaccurate – there are several other reptiles that do the same)*

13.

In Japan, teachers are not required to bow in front of the emperor. *(inaccurate – actually, nobody is)*

14.

The last new antibiotic was invented in the 1970s. Anything marketed since then is just an upgraded or fine-tuned version of existing antibiotics. *(false)*

15.

Nobody has ever seen a giant sepia alive. *(false)*

16.

Glass is a liquid and 'flows' incredibly slowly. The windows of really old buildings are thinner at the top as the glass 'flows' down due to gravity. *(false)*

17.

So far, nobody has witnessed a blue whale giving birth. *(false)*

18.

$1 000 000 banknotes exist. *(false)*

19.

When the moon gets bigger, plants grow faster. *(not proven)*

20.

Werdenberg, Switzerland is the smallest town in Europe. It has 70 residents. *(false – Hum, Croatia had a population of 21 in 2011 and is listed as the world's smallest town)*

21.

In some salmon farms, a small shark is let in intentionally in order to keep the fish alert. This is believed to improve salmon's taste. *(not proven)*

22.

In some countries, an unmarried man cannot own female goats. *(not proven)*

23.

Nails and hair continue to grow after death. *(false – they only appear longer when skin dehydrates and they protrude from the scalp and nail beds)*

24.

Dolphins save people from drowning by pushing them to the shore. *(inaccurate – in fact, dolphins play by pushing people in random directions. Naturally, only the lucky survivors can provide their account.)*

25.

Except for jelly fish, all animal bodies today have three tissue layers. *(false – thousands of species have two layers)*

26.

Leonardo da Vinci invented scissors. *(false)*

27.

There are no herbivores amongst the 10 most intelligent animal species. *(false, for instance the elephant)*

28.

Cracking your knuckles leads to arthritis. *(false, no correlation has been proven. Donald Unger cracked the knuckles of his left hand every day for 60 years but not those of his right hand. Thus, he sort of proved that cracking cannot lead to arthritis.)*

29.

A toilet's flush will change direction depending upon which hemisphere it is in. *(false)*

30.

If you cut an earthworm in half it will regenerate into two earthworms. *(false, only the front part might survive)*

31.

Goldfish have a 3 second memory. *(false, tests proved that goldfish retain memories for weeks)*

32.

All bats are blind. *(false)*

33.

Chameleons blend into their surroundings. *(false)*

34.

Vikings had horns on their helmets. *(false – the myth started in the 1870s, when Richard Wagner staged his opera cycle 'Der Ring des Nibelungen' and the costume designer made horned helmets for the Viking characters)*

35.

Humans have five senses.
(false – there are many more senses)

36.

The ancient Romans vomited in the so-called 'vomitorium'. *(false – in fact, the entrances to stadiums were called 'vomitoria')*

37.

Carrots are good for your eyes. *(deliberate disinformation – during World War II, the British military spread the rumour that carrots improved pilots' night vision, thus concealing from the Germans the use of radar. They fooled pretty much everybody.)*

38.

Mother birds will abandon babies if you touch them.
(false)

39.

Different parts of your tongue detect different tastes.
(false – do an experiment)

40.

Apple's logo is dedicated to the memory of Alan Turing, who committed suicide by eating a cyanide-poisoned apple. *(disproven by Rob Janoff, designer of the Apple logo, and by Steve Jobs)*

41.

Antibiotics should never be mixed with alcohol. *(Actually, most antibiotics do not interfere with alcohol. Historically, patients being treated for gonorrhoea were not permitted to drink for 21 days as doctors feared that if drunk, patients might be promiscuous and spread the infection.)*

42.

The test pilot of the first and top-secret US military jet aircraft P-59, Jack Woolams, wore a gorilla mask. This way, if other pilots saw and reported the aircraft, nobody would believe their story. *(not proven)*

43.

If you are left-handed, statistically, you die earlier. *(false – a very poorly done 1988 study by Diane Halpern and Stanley Coren: 'Do right-handers live longer?' spread the myth)*

44.

Up to 50% of the water on Earth arrived on the back of comets. *(false – several studies from 2014 and 2015 disprove it)*

BONUS:

I handpicked some materials from my next book, dedicated to quizzes in the popular multiple-choice format. I broadly use the 'Which is NOT true?' approach which allows you to learn two more facts by answering a single question!

The diverse list of categories includes geography, animals, history, astronomy, strange laws from around the world and many others.

QUIZ 1

Introducing the 'Which is NOT true?' approach How much do you know about the United States of America?

1.

Which is NOT true?

a) Texas ranks 5th amongst all US states by GDP.
b) John Pershing, Commander of the US Expeditionary Force in World War I, failed to stop Pancho Villa from crossing the border. Villa's troops reached the state of New Mexico before retreating.
c) Amarillo, Texas, hosts the World's Largest Calf Fry Festival. 'Calf fries' are, in fact, bull testicles.

2.

Which is NOT true?

a) Texas is the only state to have been ruled by six different nations: Spain, France, Mexico, the Republic of Texas, the Confederate States, and the USA.
b) Texas was the only state to enter the Union by treaty instead of territorial annexation.
c) The longest main street in America, 53 km (33 miles), is in Dallas, Texas.

3.

Which is NOT true?

a) Homosexual behaviour is a misdemeanour

offence in Texas.

b) In Odessa, Texas, the Star of David and the peace symbol are considered to be satanic symbols and are, thus, prohibited.

c) Texas has a larger GDP than New York and Florida combined.

4.

Which is NOT true?

a) New York City was for a while the first capital of the United States of America.

b) The people of France sent the Statue of Liberty to the American people as a present.

c) In the state of New York, you can buy wine with your groceries.

5.

Which is NOT true?

a) There is not a single Walmart store in New York City.

b) Osama Bin Laden was wanted by the FBI for the 9/11 attacks.

c) Farting in New York City churches is considered a misdemeanour.

6.

Which is NOT true?

a) New York is the state with the lowest obesity rate.
b) The 'New York Post' is the oldest running newspaper in the country.
c) In 1945, a B-25 bomber slammed into the Empire State Building.

7.

Which is NOT true?

a) George Washington owned 800 slaves and established a system that ensured that escapees were returned to their masters.
b) George Washington had to surrender once during a battle.
c) After his second term of office, George Washington ran for the US Senate.

8.

Which is NOT true?

a) The first McDonald's restaurant opened in San Bernardino, California.
b) In 1947, Norma Jean Baker, later known as Marilyn Monroe, was crowned Artichoke Queen in Castroville, California.

c) The mockingbird is California's official bird.

9.

Which is NOT true?

a) In 1862, Abraham Lincoln personally endorsed the largest mass hanging in US history, which led to the hanging of 38 Dakota Indian men in Minnesota.
b) Lincoln was the first President to shake hands instead of bow.
c) Edwin Booth, a brother of Lincoln's assassin, saved the life of President Lincoln's son in a train accident.

10.

Which is NOT true?

a) So far, Abraham Lincoln is the only President to have held a patent.
b) Lincoln was the first President to ride on a train.
c) Lincoln set up the Department of Agriculture.

ANSWERS:

1. a
2. c
3. c
4. c
5. b
6. a
7. c
8. c
9. b
10. b

QUIZ 2

How much do you know about the United States of America?

1.

Abraham Lincoln ran twice for the US Senate and

a) lost both.
b) lost the first time.
c) was successful both times.

2.

California has a bigger population than

a) the United Kingdom.
b) Canada.
c) Germany.

3.

Which state(s) are larger than California in terms of territory?

a) Alaska.
b) Alaska and Montana.
c) Alaska and Texas.

4.

California was initially named the Grizzly Bear State. When there were no bears left, it became the

a) Golden State.
b) Silver State.
c) Gem State.

5.

George Washington set a record by pronouncing his inaugural address in less than

a) 2 minutes.
b) 5 minutes.
c) 10 minutes.

6.

Abraham Lincoln

a) had no middle name and actually hated being called Abe.
b) tried vigorously to conceal the fact that his middle name was 'Molly'.
c) simply had the letter 'B' instead of a middle name.

7.

George Washington was inaugurated in two different cities: New York City and

a) Washington D.C.
b) Philadelphia.
c) Baltimore.

8.

There are more prisoners in the USA than there are

a) teachers.

b) civil servants.
c) farmers.

9.

New York City has a bigger population than

a) 50% of US states.
b) 65% of US states.
c) 80% of US states.

10.

'Don't mess with Texas' appeared first in 1986 as

a) an anti-litter slogan.
b) an election slogan.
c) a Chuck Norris quote.

ANSWERS:

1. a
2. b
3. c
4. a
5. a
6. a
7. b
8. c
9. c
10. a

QUIZ 3

How much do you know about the world?

1.

Arabic numerals actually originated in

a) China.
b) India.
c) Persia.

2.

In 1967, a country in Europe changed its street traffic directionality from left (UK style) to right (continental style). The very first day, traffic was a total mess. It happened in

a) Ireland.
b) Sweden.
c) Liechtenstein.

3.

Molotov cocktails were named after

a) an actual Soviet minister of foreign affairs.
b) their inventor.
c) a Soviet guerrilla commander who first used one.

4.

The NATO member without an army is

a) Costa Rica.
b) Switzerland.
c) Iceland.

5.

In our solar system, there is only one planet that turns clockwise. It is

a) Mercury.
b) Venus.
c) Jupiter.

6.

The word 'dreamt' is peculiar because

a) in English, it is the only one (excluding derivatives) that ends with 'mt'.
b) Grammar experts want this form abolished and changed to 'dreamed'.
c) the majority of US first-graders spell it wrong.

7.

Many Chinese women wear bathing suits that cover their face. Why?

a) They are afraid of local parasites.
b) They are ashamed of their body and don't want to be recognised.
c) In China, suntan on the face is often associated with peasantry and is, therefore, undesirable.

8.

Which animal has fingerprints that cannot be easily distinguished from human ones?

a) Panda.
b) Koala.
c) Racoon.

9.

What do Yoda and Miss Piggy have in common?

a) The voices of Yoda and Miss Piggy were done by the same person.
b) The puppets were produced by the same company.
c) Yoda means 'pig' in Zulu dialect.

10.

Rudolf, Santa's reindeer, is depicted wrong in most Christmas pictures and movies. Why?

a) The shape of the nose.
b) The shape of the hooves.
c) Rudolf has to be a girl. Male reindeer lose their antlers before Christmas, while females do not.

ANSWERS:

1. b
2. b
3. a
4. c
5. b
6. a
7. c
8. b
9. a
10. c

QUIZ 4

How much do you know about the world?

1.

Pandas are the most expensive animal in a zoo. The second most expensive animals are

a) elephants.
b) rhinoceroses.
c) lions.

2.

One African country has far more pyramids than Egypt. It is

a) Sudan.
b) Ethiopia.
c) Morocco.

3.

Until 2011, beer was not considered an alcoholic drink in

a) Germany.
b) Russia.
c) Czech Republic.

4.

In some districts of which European country is flushing the toilet after 10 pm against the law?

a) Belarus.

b) Switzerland.
c) Moldova.

5.

Neckties were first used in

a) Croatia.
b) France.
c) Italy.

6.

Women or larger-than-cat female animals are not allowed in one part of which European country?

a) Hungary.
b) Wales.
c) Greece.

7.

In 1712, there was a 30 February in

a) Sweden.
b) The Netherlands.
c) The Russian Empire.

8.

Which country has four official languages and uses none of them on its postage stamps?

a) Aruba.

b) Chile.
c) Switzerland.

9.

Nodding your head expresses 'yes' in the vast majority of cultures. Be careful though, it means 'no' in

a) Sweden.
b) Finland.
c) Bulgaria.

10.

Ford Pinto was not a success in Brazil. 'Pinto' in local slang means a

a) 'small penis'.
b) 'small brain'.
c) 'small biceps'.

ANSWERS:

1. a
2. a
3. b
4. b
5. a
6. c
7. a
8. c
9. c
10. a

NOTE ON SOURCES AND DESCRIPTION OF THE VERIFICATION PROCESS

Sources

It was originally my intention to include a bibliography of all of the sources I used to verify the facts. However, after the sources began to number in the hundreds, I decided instead to publish everything online. Additionally, for a great number of the facts I provide you with links for further reading.

Should you like to know more, please visit ***https://www.raiseyourbrain.com/1123-hard-to-believe-facts-book-sources***

There, you will also have the possibility to subscribe to my newsletter and to learn about new projects before everyone else!

Verification process

To start with, however a great read Wikipedia is, I never use it to confirm facts; I rather checked the sources listed there and evaluated them instead. Anything science-related like 'Sometimes Pluto is closer to Earth than Neptune' or 'Water is densest at 4°C (39.2°F)' would need to be confirmed by at least two (preferably three) separate scientific publications, be it on paper or online of the sort of http://www.science.gov/,

http://www.nasa.gov/,
http://www.britannica.com/,
http://www.sciencemag.org/,
https://www.newscientist.com/,
https://www.genome.gov/education/,
http://www.howstuffworks.com/,
http://www.merriam-webster.com/.

The scientific publications and websites of the best universities worldwide are also consistently checked (excerpt from the list):
University of Cambridge,
Stanford University,
University of Oxford,
California Institute of Technology,
Massachusetts Institute of Technology,
Harvard University,
Princeton University,
Imperial College London,
ETH Zurich – Swiss Federal Institute of Technology,
Yale University,
Columbia University,
University of Toronto,
Humboldt University of Berlin,
University of Tokyo,
Heidelberg University,
University of Melbourne,

Peking University etc.

For events or facts of the type ‘The 46th Vice President of the United States, Dick Cheney, shot a man in the face and the victim apologised’, I checked at least three reputable newspaper articles and/or confirmed television reports. Example for newspapers / TV channels used to verify events: The New York Times, Washington Post, Wall Street Journal, The Guardian, The Economist, Financial Times, Times of India, Le Monde, The Sydney Morning Herald, Frankfurter Allgemeine Zeitung, Bloomberg, Al Jazeera, Reuters, Associated Press, BBC, TV5 MONDE, CNN, etc.

If there is only one source or if the sources were deemed not reliable, I simply discarded the fact. Exception: when NASA says that there is liquid water on Mars, I take this first-hand information as plausible. Cross-checking is not possible for the time being as all other sources also quote NASA.

ACKNOWLEDGEMENTS

This book is dedicated to my family: my loving wife Anna, my curious and restless sons Pavel and Nikolay, and my mother Maria, who sparked my interest in reading. Thank you for being so patient with me during the lengthy process of writing. You are my inspiration!

Many thanks to the editor Jonathon Tabet; the illustrator Yuliya Krumova; to all test readers, friends, and colleagues who provided vital feedback and constructive criticism.

I am truly impressed by the Kickstarter community which not only was great in the crowdfunding part but also provided guidance and shared precious experience.

I hope you have enjoyed this book. I would greatly appreciate it if you would write your honest review on Amazon and/or on GoodReads:

https://www.amazon.com/1123-Hard-Believe-Facts-RaiseYourBrain-com-ebook/dp/B01GQRGE6E

https://www.goodreads.com/book/show/30522577-1123-hard-to-believe-facts

ABOUT THE AUTHOR

Born in Bulgaria, I have lived in places like Germany Belgium and Iraq, before settling down with my family in Luxembourg. With varied interests, I have always suffered from an insatiable appetite for facts stemming from an unrestrainable intellectual curiosity. It has certainly influenced my academic background and career after acquiring Master degrees in Greek Philology German and English Translation, I graduated in Crisis Management and Diplomacy and, most recently, undertook an MBA.

My career has been equally broad and diverse, swinging from that of an army paratrooper and a military intelligence analyst; through to that of a civil servant with the European Commission, and presently, that of a clerk, performing purely financial tasks in a major bank.

Member of MENSA.

1123 HARD TO BELIEVE FACTS
first edition

Author: Nayden Kostov
Editor: Jonathon Tabet
Design: Yuliya Krumova
Format: 5,25 x 8

ISBN-13: 978-9995998011
ISBN-10: 9995998017

57063355R00150

Made in the USA
Lexington, KY
05 November 2016